THE ART OF
MONEY
WORKBOOK

THE ART OF
MONEY
WORKBOOK

A Three-Step Plan to Transform
Your Relationship with Money

BARI TESSLER

SHAMBHALA

Shambhala Publications, Inc.
2129 13th Street
Boulder, Colorado 80302
www.shambhala.com

Cover art: Galyna_P/Shutterstock
Cover design: Daniel Urban-Brown
Interior design: Allison Meierding

9 8 7 6 5 4 3 2 1

First edition
Printed in China

♾ This edition is printed on acid-free paper that meets the American
National Standards Institute Z39.48 Standard.
♻ Shambhala Publications makes every effort to print on recycled paper.
For more information please visit www.shambhala.com.
Shambhala Publications is distributed worldwide by Penguin Random
House, Inc., and its subsidiaries.

Library of Congress Cataloging-in-Publication Data
Names: Tessler, Bari, author.
Title: The art of money workbook: a three-step plan to transform
your relationship with money / Bari Tessler.
Description: Boulder, Colorado: Shambhala, 2022.
Identifiers: LCCN 2021020389 | ISBN 9781611808445
(trade paperback)
Subjects: LCSH: Money—Psychological aspects. | Finance,
Personal—Psychological aspects. | Self-help techniques.
Classification: LCC HG222.3 .T4753 2022 | DDC 332.024—dc23
LC record available at https://lccn.loc.gov/2021020389

Contents

Welcome

Dear Money Adventurer,

Welcome to a new journey—a unique opportunity to explore, grow, and discover. Wherever you are on your personal money path, I am so excited to have you here. However hesitant, nervous, excited, or curious you may be—all are welcome. You've taken a brave first step, and I'm proud of you.

I hope this workbook will become your celebration—an initiation to new levels of self-growth and understanding. May this be the beginning of a vibrantly meaningful and deeply personal journey that brings more creativity, pleasure, and self-expression to your days.

If you're reading this, you might have noticed a stirring in the shadows, a gentle voice whispering that there is more to money and how you interact with it than meets the eye. Maybe you came to be here very intentionally, consciously pursuing a new, more meaningful way to engage with money in your life. Or perhaps you're wondering why you're even reading this—you feel a little uncertain—but you're still here.

This workbook is more than just another self-help tool. This money work has the potential to carry us deeper than we expect—beyond personal finances and into the realm of knowing ourselves more authentically and more intimately. Here we forgive, we let go, and we celebrate. Here we choose to write new chapters with intention and compassion. Here we discover untold depths to the saga of our lives and go deep soul diving to empower our hopes, dreams, and aspirations.

Let this workbook be your vehicle for a new adventure—equipped with the tools and resources to forge a new path and travel forward with confidence and trust. Here we will build the framework you need to create genuine, sustainable change in your relationship with money.

> This is a calling-in.
> We don't believe in tough love here.
> You are where you are right now,
> and I am honored to meet you there.

More than that, know that every page of this workbook is steeped in love, like the coziest cup of tea on a gloomy day. The work we do here is founded on grace and compassion—it pairs well with dark chocolate and tender loving care. We aren't here just to manage your finances, though we'll do that, too! You'll get to decide what you want the next chapter in your Money Story to look like, and you'll learn how to write it—and how to own every step along the way.

Here you will find gentle encouragement, practical tools and resources, new avenues for creativity and joy, and an abundance of support.

Here's to you, Money Adventurer, and this new beginning.

Onward.

With much love and dark chocolate,

THE ART OF
MONEY
WORKBOOK

The Art of Money will help anyone transform their relationship with money and, in so doing, transform their life. When we dare to speak the truth about money, amazing healing begins.

Introduction

I'm so excited to share the adventure of the *Art of Money Workbook* with you! Here, we choose to travel with gentleness and compassion. Tough love may be effective in some situations, but for most of us, this approach leaves us wanting to stick our heads in the sand and hide.

Maybe we've tried tough love already—so many of the traditional money books take that approach—but have been left feeling like crap. Or we've ignored this area of life altogether—it's not like we were ever taught to talk about it. But hoping it would magically take care of itself isn't helping. Or maybe you find yourself somewhere in between these places, curious but hesitant.

Yet, here you are, ready to step into your money emotions and dive deeper into your Money Story. I invite you to bring curiosity and care to this journey.

The compassionate path is far, far more
effective in creating sustainable transformation
than the self-critical one.

WHY EXPLORE YOUR RELATIONSHIP TO MONEY ANYWAY?

When I received my master's degree in somatic psychology in 1998, I thought my work as a therapist would focus on themes of body, sexuality, food, intimacy, grief, and death—the big touchstones in life. While my work does incorporate each of these topics, I have chosen instead to *use our relationship with money as a gateway to self-awareness and a training ground for compassion, confidence, and self-worth.*

My own money journey began when my student loan came due when I was in my late twenties. With a flash of fear and confusion, it dawned on me that financial literacy had not been a part of my studies—not in graduate school, college, high school, and not at all growing up . . . And the shame really started to seep in. I was shocked and completely unprepared. I had no idea how I was going to start my own business or handle my bookkeeping, never mind feel comfortable talking about money with my clients or help couples work through challenging financial dynamics.

Sure, I had learned some bits and pieces. But I did not know how to have a healthy relationship with money, manage my money, or understand all the emotions I felt during daily money interactions. This all snapped sharply into focus when I was confronted with the reality of my student loan payments, but it took me a little while to realize that I wasn't alone.

Most of us never got the financial education we needed as children and young adults. The vast majority of folks I know did not receive a financial education at all—through grade school into adulthood. Money wasn't talked about or seemed to spark nothing but fighting and heartbreak. Is it any wonder we're confused, ashamed, and silent?

Fast-forward a few years, and I had decided to learn everything I could about money management, starting with bookkeeping. I ran a bookkeeping business for a few years, working with therapists, coaches, and artists. I learned more about people's money relationships, spending patterns, and financial dynamics managing their books than if I had spent hours in therapy with these folks.

Money isn't just about the numbers;
it's also about our relationship with
ourselves—and each other.

Let that sink in.

I created my three-phase financial therapy methodology, the Art of Money (AOM), in a tiny cabin deep in the woods when I was first living with my husband. I needed a framework, something I could share to encourage and support my clients on their own money journeys. I spent hours in those woods—seeking, praying, and pleading with the trees for the piece I could feel was missing. Eventually, I returned to our ridiculously tiny cabin to map out the methodology I have taught ever since.

And the Art of Money was born.

I've been teaching my financial therapy methodology for over two decades now. I developed this curriculum by instructing small groups over and over—fine-tuning, adjusting, and course-correcting as I went. The more I dove into the work, the more I stretched, grew, and discovered in my own money journey. I experienced shifts in my relationships I would never have anticipated—genuine, healthy change that brought new depths of love and intimacy to my life. Once again, as so many times before, I felt a gentle calling, a whisper of inspiration unfolding.

After years of tweaking and recalibrating, connecting and sharing, there was another story begging to be told. My book *The Art of Money— A Life-Changing Guide to Financial Happiness* is filled with personal experiences and stories from the AOM community, sharing how each of us uses these life-changing tools every day.

This workbook is the next evolution in the Art of Money.

Here is a private place to root your explorations. Here you will find gentle prompts, questions, quotes, and teachings from the Art of Money. These exercises will help you illuminate some of the deeper terrain as you explore your money journey and the emotions that come up within your Money Story. You can use this workbook on its own, guiding you down the unfolding path of your relationship with money, or you can pair it with my book for a little extra tender loving care and perspective along the way. This is your journey, and the only "right way" is the one that works for you.

A note here, before we carry on. By its very nature, money work is intensely personal—no two people travel the exact same path. Before we embark on this journey together, it is crucial to acknowledge that we live in a society where personal privilege, or lack of it, underwrites our experiences as we grow through life. Whether we realize it or not, it is through this lens that we view and interact with the world around us. Your personal experiences of value, accessibility, support, and exclusion shape and inform your relationship with money—consciously and unconsciously.

As we move through this work together, we will need to do some unpacking. No matter who you are or what your relationship with money is like right now, there will be some heavy lifting to do. There will also be unexpected gifts and joyful celebrations. Here we break down what isn't ours to carry, we release the past, and we step forward into a new chapter of intimacy, growth, and self-care. Here we become the author of our own stories and builder of our deepest dreams. I will always lead with compassion, tenderness, and love. Give yourself permission to treat this work as a gentle invitation into self-reflection.

Let's get to know this money terrain, together . . . On our journey, you'll bring your financial goals, unique money narratives, and a good pair of galoshes. I'll bring practical tools, a wealth of therapeutic experience, loving encouragement, and inspiration galore. I know these woods like the back of my hand and will show the way with vision, heart, and playfulness.

We'll begin with some of the Art of Money teachings that will pave the way as we embark on this journey together. So, dear Money Adventurer, grab yourself a cozy cuppa, some scrumptious dark chocolate, and your favorite pen.

Let the journey begin!

GENTLENESS, COMPASSION, LOVE

Here we let go of "tough love" and give "soft love" a chance.
Leave your shoulds, shouldn'ts, and why-can't-I's at the door.
They have no place on this healing journey.
There is nothing heroic about self-criticism.
Grace yourself with forgiveness.
Above all else, please be gentle with yourself.
This is your path to carve, your story to write.
Make it luxurious, loving, and sweet.

MY THREE-PHASE MONEY THERAPY METHODOLOGY FOR BIG SHIFTS IN YOUR RELATIONSHIP TO MONEY

Whether we acknowledge it or not, money impacts every area of our lives. Most of us were never taught how to engage authentically with our money, so we wind up repeating piecemeal interactions without a thought that there might be something deeper to these exchanges. This restricted perspective leaves us living out a fractured pattern: we stick our heads in the sand and abdicate our power to write a different chapter in our Money Story.

In this workbook, we will explore three levels of steps we must engage with to create a genuine shift in our relationship to money. These levels are interconnected but with each one opening a new realm to explore and engage with your money. Here, we will equip you with the tools you need to sustain you along your journey.

We aren't here to skim the surface. Money work is deeply personal, intimately revelatory, even life-changing—if you're willing. The three phases outlined below provide the framework you need to establish healthy, sustainable change in your relationship with money—guiding your journey and providing touchstones along the way.

1. **Money Healing**

   Here we discover the Money Story we've been unconsciously writing all of our lives. This is where we do the emotional work of creating a truly genuine relationship with money. We dissolve shame, release guilt, and uncover precious gifts we had previously overlooked. We unearth all the patterns we've inherited from our family of origin, lineage, and culture. We bring gentle curiosity and compassion to identify and unwind patterns that no longer serve us. We claim our value. We learn emotional and body-based tools to help us lean into support and growth. We breathe deeply, incorporating self-care, acceptance, and love every step of the way.

2. Money Practices

Here we focus on the practical—number crunching, systems, and habits of building an ongoing, clear-eyed, supportive relationship with money. We establish personal Money Practices to engage with our numbers on a new level, empowering ourselves to go deeper by learning to take ourselves on Money Dates. Here we gather data and learn the language of money. We align these practices with our deepest values, creating playful, personally meaningful, life-affirming interactions with our money.

Buh-bye dull, dusty budget. Hellooooo, values-based bookkeeping!

3. Money Maps

This is where we go deep soul diving into the big picture of our hopes, dreams, goals, and aspirations—how they're unfolding and how money can fuel them. In this realm, we learn how to make great money decisions and align our choices with our personal values. We embrace conscious spending. We learn to reframe our perspective and identify how money can best support our lives as we grow and change over time. In this space, we explore the legacy we want to leave behind.

Each phase is always happening; woven together, each one affects the other.

Think of these three phases as interconnected doorways to financial transformation. At any time, you can step through and explore a new level of money work.

This is our journey, and these are the paths we will explore in this workbook.

Welcome to the beginning of a new journey, Money Adventurer.

Here we explore the vast terrain of our hearts with compassionate, loving awareness.

We dissolve shame and unwind old patterns that no longer serve us.

It is time to claim our value, heal, forgive, and celebrate.

My, oh my, do we celebrate!

This deeply personal, inner work is our foundation.

Deep breath, dear Adventurer . . . and let the healing begin.

PHASE ONE

MONEY
HEALING

1

What Does Your Body Have to Say about Money— And Why Should You Care?

Since the beginning of my money work, I have introduced some basic somatic—or body-based—tools to our Art of Money community.

Soma = Body

Somatic work brings more understanding, health, and peace to our relationship with money. It offers awareness and enables us to self-soothe, support ourselves, and choose new patterns and behaviors to transform our relationship with money.

For me, personally, somatic practices have saved my life and changed the way I move through the world. This work has helped me learn how to get out of my head and ground myself in my body. I had to make a conscious effort to learn how to identify different sensations and emotions and experience how they felt in my body. Along the way, I began to truly listen to my body and understand the messages my body was trying to share with me. This life-changing experience is what led me to pursue my master's degree in somatic psychology. I knew that I needed to find out more, to learn to understand and apply somatic practices on a deeper level so that I could work to share these tools with others.

This awareness has truly helped me in every area of my life, from being a partner and half of a couple to parenting, the work I do in the world, my own relationship with money—the list goes on and on.

So many of us have mindfulness practices in other areas of life, on the yoga mat, in conversation with our sweetie, or while eating, yet we neglect to bring this same awareness to money. When confronted with an overdue tax bill, we tend to get scattered, overwhelmed, panicked, or numb—which might feel like a racing heart, butterflies in your stomach, or a sudden need to do or think about anything else.

Using somatic practices within our money relationship brings us into the shining spotlight of awareness. They can help us self-regulate, ground, and resource—aiding us in choosing a new pathway out of old patterns. Here we find the physical balance to our soul-deep journey.

The integration of money work and somatic practices is such a profound tool for transformation that I simply cannot imagine one without the other.

When life gets tough, it's tempting to escape
our experience by checking out of our bodies.
But trust me: the answers are never out there.
The way out . . . is always in.

2

Money Emotions

Let's start by talking about all the different money emotions that come up in our daily lives.

Money emotions are a normal part of being human. For better or worse, money is connected to our survival instincts, identity, self-worth, and tons of deep-seated personal stuff. It's no wonder money triggers such big and instinctive reactions! And it's also no surprise that *fear*—whether expressed by fight, flight, or freeze—can come up so often in big and small money moments.

But other emotions come up around money, too . . . in spades.

From shame, anxiety, anger, guilt, and sadness to joy, excitement, hope, and confidence—and everywhere in between—understanding our personal money emotions is an essential life skill.

Learning to name these emotions, feel these emotions, and move them through our bodies is also an essential life and money skill.

You see, money work isn't about *getting rid* of our emotions around financial matters and all their connections to the rest of our big, messy, glorious lives, but learning to *respond* to them. I know, I know. A lot of the emotions we feel about money are really uncomfortable. You might just want to shut down and make them *stop*. If we want to break out of that cycle, though, we need to learn how to acknowledge our emotions, notice them in our bodies, and sit with those feelings without pushing them away.

This is a loving reminder that wading into our money emotions is a big deal—this work is intensely personal.

Please be gentle with yourself as you take this brave step forward.

Remember, there is no rush here, no hurry to "get it done." There are also no "right answers," and you don't have to take all this on at once.

So steep yourself a cozy cuppa and take a deep breath. Give yourself permission to go at your own pace and honor your own timing. You are safe here, and we'll begin whenever you're ready.

CORE EMOTIONS

○ Anger	○ Grief
○ Anxiety	○ Guilt
○ Calmness	○ Joy
○ Curiosity	○ Overwhelm
○ Disappointment	○ Pride
○ Disgust	○ Sadness
○ Empowerment	○ Security
○ Excitement	○ Shame
○ Fear	○ Surprise
○ Gratefulness	○ Tenderness

What is the main emotion that comes up for you around money? What emotion—or combination or cocktail of emotions—do you see frequently?

What money emotion did we miss?

What about the other end of the money emotion spectrum? If you gravitated more toward "negative" emotions, what "positive" emotions can you identify with?

Take some time to explore these now.

Pause for a moment and try to think about your last three money interactions. How did each one feel?

When you were checking out at the grocery store or exchanging money for goods or services in some other way, what emotions popped up? Shame? Anger? Fear? Guilt? Joy? Sadness? Happiness? Write down what you can remember.

MONEY INTERACTION #1:

What money emotions came up? Where do you feel them? How do they sit in your body?

MONEY INTERACTION #2:

What money emotions came up? Where do you feel them? How do they sit in your body?

MONEY INTERACTION #3:

What money emotions came up? Where do you feel them? How do they sit in your body?

Go gently here. Explore with compassion.

Trust that you are safe. Make space for your emotions.

Stay present with your feelings when they come up.

Recognize and name your feelings sooner.

Soothe yourself in the moment.

Gently move your emotions to the side, so you can think more clearly.

Break down big issues into manageable bits.

Stay curious and open to new possibilities.

Even after all these years, challenging emotions still arise for me when I'm faced with something new or big around money.

Here's how to know you're getting somewhere with money work: when a difficult emotion comes up but you have reliable tools to soothe yourself, self-regulate, and keep going.

You *can* say "hello" and give your shame some space. Move it gently to the side. Offer it tea and chocolate. Notice and observe. Calm your nervous system so that fight-flight-freeze isn't overwhelming your entire body. Start a dialogue with yourself; ask new questions with gentle curiosity.

Emotions aren't your enemy. Even the challenging ones have important messages and gifts to share when it comes to money. Our goal isn't to make those emotions vanish. Even if we could—we can't—we would miss out on so much beautiful awareness and wisdom.

My hope is that you learn to use these tools and get the support you need to sit with your money emotions. On that note, here's the first tool that I want to share with you.

I teach this over and over and over. It's that good.

3

The Body Check-In

The Body Check-In is my absolute favorite tool for conscious money work. It supports us along steep learning curves and through deep, inner exploration . . . It's the perfect foundational tool to empower you *right now*.

The Body Check-In is the cornerstone of my work. I return to it repeatedly because of its simplicity, elegance, and profound power to support us through challenging emotions and stressful situations.

This practice creates space for us to mentally step back and consider our situation rather than reacting impulsively. The Body Check-In teaches us to slow down and notice our emotions, sensations, and breath during our daily money interactions. With patience and sincere practice, this exercise will expand into a deeper awareness and understanding, changing our money interactions and conversations.

I invite my students to practice this exercise over and over, before money interactions, during money conversations, and again afterward—like a debriefing after a covert mission. While I have gotten some eye rolls when I first mention the Body Check-In practice, many students have come back to tell me that this tool was truly life-changing for them.

This simple tool really can move mountains. I've seen it happen again and again.

BODY CHECK-IN PROMPTS

The Body Check-In starts with a pause. Stop whatever you're doing. Take a moment for yourself. Gather up all of your attention and turn your gaze inward.

Take a few slow, deep breaths. Close your eyes if that feels helpful to you. Adopt an attitude of openness and curiosity without judgment or any attempt to change anything. Simply notice.

Start with your physical sensations. Become aware of how your body feels on your chair or how your feet rest on the ground. Notice sensations of movement and stillness, the breeze across your skin, or the quiet stability of your pelvis. Notice how your breath feels, moving in and out—is it deep, shallow, cool, tight?

Next, gently observe the emotions moving through you. Do you feel angry, anxious, annoyed, or bewildered? How do these emotions feel in your body? Is your jaw set in hot determination, or do you sense a flutter of excitement in your belly? Allow yourself to simply be aware of these emotions and how they are being expressed in your body.

Also, notice any thoughts, images, memories, or self-talk. There's no need to cling to them or push them away—simply acknowledge them. Are self-criticism, judgment, or other challenging sensations arising? Notice. Are joy, excitement, or other expansive sensations coming up for you? Notice these, too.

As you scan your body, emotions, and mind, **ask yourself if there's anything you'd like to remove from or add to this moment.** If you notice your jaw is tight, perhaps you'd like to wiggle it loose. If you notice your breath is shallow and quick, you might gently lengthen and deepen it. Come home to your body. Follow your breath. It isn't about perfecting or even changing anything. Here, it is simply about being aware.

After you complete a Body Check-In, ask yourself these questions and write down your responses—remembering to adopt an attitude of open, compassionate curiosity.

What do you notice on a physical level? How does your body feel right now? What sensations are present in your body?

What emotions are present?

What is your breath doing? Where is it in your body? Are you breathing deeply, shallowly, smoothly?

If you have any thoughts arising, what are they?

What are you learning about yourself?

What's one thing you can do right now to support yourself?

If your jaw is tight, would it feel good to loosen it a little? Could you adjust yourself in your chair to be a bit more comfortable? Can you wiggle your shoulders a little?

That's it! You just did your first Body Check-In.

When we slow down and trust the body's wisdom,
it will reveal to us what we need most.

Once you've completed your first Body Check-In, then *repeat, repeat, repeat.* I recommend revisiting this practice before, during, and after every money decision.

WHERE CAN YOU USE A BODY CHECK-IN?

Bring the Body Check-In to the grocery store with you and to money conversations with your partner/spouse. Access it when you're looking at your online balances, paying bills, and reviewing your numbers. Try it out when you make your money decisions. Bring the Body Check-In into as many daily money interactions as you can, and you will transform your relationship to money in a beautiful way. Take time for a Body Check-In with any of the money decisions you face throughout your day, from teensy to monumental. Think of it as a compassionate treasure hunt—you may find clues, patterns, or insights about whatever you're feeling.

The Body Check-In is a tool we will call on repeatedly as you delve into the deep and sometimes turbulent waters of Money Healing, work your way through your Money Story, or take yourself on a Money Date. But don't worry: we're going to be doing all these things together in this workbook.

BODY CHECK-INS

Exercise #1: Before Money Interaction

I felt . . .

My thoughts, intuitions, realizations . . .

Exercise #2: During Money Interaction

I felt . . .

My thoughts, intuitions, realizations . . .

Exercise #3: After Money Interaction

I felt . . .

My thoughts, intuitions, realizations . . .

It can take some time and patience to learn how to work with your emotions around money. It can get uncomfortable and even scary at times. The level of grief and trauma in our bodies and histories will determine if we need more in-depth support with a private somatic therapist or somatic-trauma therapist or if books or courses are sufficient. Many of us need both. That's why working with a somatic therapist, financial therapist, or other trusted guide can be so helpful: the support allows you to develop more and more tools to stay in your body, listen to it, and work with those strong, challenging emotions.

You are not broken—being human is just messy sometimes.

4

Delving into Your
Personal Money Story

Close your eyes. What is your earliest memory of money?

Your Money Story is the saga of your relationship with money—the pain, the joy, and the learning. It is the unconscious narrative that you have been weaving all of your life, and your experiences are as unique as you are.

It includes all of the facts of your past financial life, the emotional wounds and triumphs, the tough conversations.

The beliefs and habits inherited from your parents and lineage, the ways you adopted them, and the ways you rebelled against or even transcended them are there too.

It includes your strengths and challenges with money arising from your unique circumstances, wiring, and personality type and all of the sensations, emotions, and bodily reactions that money stirs within you.

Your Money Story is the whole shebang—past and present. And you probably never even realized that you were writing it at all.

Getting to know your Money Story is courageous, vulnerable work.

Most of us aren't conscious of our Money Story—or at least, most of it. Still, whether we look it in the eye or not, it is there: running like silent software in the background of everything we do—driving decisions, fueling fear, and whispering hypnotic half-truths we can't reason with.

When people first start looking at their Money Story, many feel a lot of shame, fear, or other difficult money emotions. As we pull our Money Story out of the closet, with all its secrecy and silence, it's easy to focus on the bad stuff. You need to know that we all have challenges *and* strengths around money—our Money Stories contain traumas *and* triumphs, pain *and* joy.

Becoming intimately familiar with our Money Story means looking at, understanding, and honoring *all* of this. Does that sound hard? It is.

But the more honest we get about our Money Story, the more empowered we are in creating *real*, lasting transformation.

> As conscious adults, when we bring these early money memories into focus, we can choose how to care for them.

If there's one thing I've learned over the years, it's that our past does not have to define our future—*especially* when it comes to our Money Stories.

You have the power to write new chapters.

It takes some work, but it is *oh*, so worth it. And we'll begin doing that here.

Treat these questions as gentle invitations into self-reflection.

This isn't like one of those forms you race through at the DMV or doctor's office. There's no need to rush here. Soak up these questions. Light a candle as you answer them if you like. Carry them out into nature with you. Take a moment to roll them around inside of you before responding.

Make this exploration and writing process an investment in your self-care—and make it really feel that way, too.

Notice what comes up for you here: memories, images, physical sensations, beliefs. Follow tangents, if that feels right. Treat these prompts like gentle little springboards into your inner landscape and your money relationship.

Tread gently here. This process can kick up a lot of emotional material, so honor your own rhythm and allow yourself to go at your own pace.

Remember to do a Body Check-In before you start working with these questions, anytime you encounter challenging emotions during this exercise, and before you move on to whatever comes next in your day after you're finished.

PRESENT MOMENT—CLARIFYING YOUR RELATIONSHIP WITH MONEY

How would you describe your relationship with money?

What are your strengths around your relationship with money? What really works for you in this area? Where do you rock with money? What are you proud of?

Where is there room for improvement in your relationship to money? What immediately springs to mind for you here? How does it feel in your body?

Now let's go deeper.

Your Relationship to Making/Earning Money

How do you make money? Is it easy? Is it challenging? Has it changed in the recent economic climate? Is your income level consistent or does it vary over time?

Do you enjoy your work? How do you feel about it?

Have you found your calling? How does that feel? If not, how does that feel—do you have any sense of how you might find it?

If you have found your calling, is it in alignment with your values? If it is, how does that feel? If it's not, how does that feel? Are you prioritizing income over alignment with your values, and is that OK for now?

Your Relationship to Spending Money

Are you comfortable spending money? Or do you feel cautious and restrained about letting yourself spend?

How does it feel when you spend? How does it feel when you don't?

What do you typically spend money on? What don't you spend money on? How do you make those decisions?

When money comes in, do you spend most or all of it right away?

Do you ever plan for your spending? Have you ever tried budgeting? How did/does that go for you?

Your Relationship to Giving Money

When do you give money? To whom and why? How often? How does it feel?

When do you not give?

How much do you give? How do you decide? Is fear part of the process? How about excitement or other emotions?

Do you give gifts or donations to charity? Are there certain conditions surrounding when you do? Do gifts or donations feel different than giving money?

Do you pay for meals or other things for friends or family? How does it feel? If you don't pay for others, would you like to?

Is there a deeper level of meaning for you about what giving is?

Your Relationship to Receiving Money

Have you ever been given money as an adult? If so, how much and from whom?

Is there someone you wish would give you money? Why and how much?

How does it feel to receive money? Do you have any sense of entitlement? What about guilt, embarrassment, or feeling undeserving? If you've never received money, how do you imagine it would feel?

In what ways does receiving money support you, and in what ways might it not?

If you have received money, does that influence you in terms of you giving money?

Your Relationship to Borrowing Money

How do you feel about borrowing money? How often do you do it? How much do you borrow?

Do you borrow from friends or family? Through credit card accounts and other loans? Through mortgages and home equity loans?

Is there a limit to how much you would borrow? How do you decide that?

Your Relationship to Loaning Money

Do you loan money? To whom and under what conditions? How much?

If you do loan, what motivates you to do so? Is it generosity? Are there feelings of guilt or of wanting to be liked?

Have you ever considered just giving the money instead of loaning it? Have you ever set up a payment plan with your borrower?

Your Relationship to Saving Money
Do you save money? What does saving money mean to you? If you do it, how does it feel? How much do you save? Why? When and under what conditions? Is it just a nice idea that you haven't quite gotten to yet?

If you do save, how long is it before you typically spend it? Do you spend it so quickly that it doesn't really count as savings?

What do you save for? Are there specific things? What's the biggest motivator for you to save? Or, if you don't save, what do you think could motivate you to do so?

Can you see any deeper features of your Money Story or your worldview that influence how you feel and behave around saving? For example, do you tend to think about the long-term future? If you do, is this born of thoughtful foresight, fear, or some mix of the two?

Your Relationship to Investing Money
Have you ever invested money? Do you do so actively now? Why or why not? What emotions come up for you around this subject?

If you invest, how does it feel when your investments grow or shrink in value?

How do you decide what to invest in? Do you have a broker or financial advisor direct you? Do you do any research for yourself? Do your values— social, political, environmental—come into play at all?

If you don't invest, would you like to in the future? What would it take for you to start?

YOUR PERSONAL MONEY HISTORY—
REFLECTION PROMPTS

Understanding that everyone's experience of family is different, if any questions feel irrelevant or don't represent your upbringing, please skip them and journey onward.

Where did you spend your childhood? What were your settings and surroundings? Was this place urban, rural, suburban? A big city or small town? Did you live in an apartment, a house, a trailer, or something else? Did your family rent or own? Did your family move around a lot? Did you spend your entire childhood in one home?

What did you learn about money from your family? What messages about money did they transmit to you—either spoken aloud or shared nonverbally through attitudes and behavior? Who played what role in your family's finances?

In what ways are you repeating your mother's role, relationship, or messages around money? In what ways have you rebelled against her patterns and gone the opposite direction? How have you worked through her patterns or broken them entirely?

In what ways are you repeating your father's role, relationship, or messages around money? In what ways have you rebelled against his patterns and gone the opposite direction? How have you worked through his patterns or broken them entirely?

What about your grandparents? Or anyone else involved in raising you? Answer these same questions around what you learned about money from them.

If you had siblings, what roles did they play in the family around money? Common roles include the spender, the saver, the confidante, the good child, and the rebel—but feel free to identify any that feel right to you. Did you play similar roles around money in your family, or did you each have different roles? What about now, as adults? Are your siblings still playing those same roles?

Were you treated differently from your siblings regarding money? How so?

What are your lineage and ethnicity? How did the culture and/or countries your family or ancestors came from impact the money messages you received as a child?

Were you raised with a religion or spirituality? What were the money messages that came along with it? What view of money was conveyed in your scriptures or teachings? Where did money fit in a spiritual life?

As a child, did you think you were rich, poor, middle class? How did that feel? Have you carried any of those feelings with you into adulthood and your current Money Story?

Have you experienced any painful events surrounding money in your life? How did they impact your money relationship and your attitudes, beliefs, and behaviors around money?

Have you had big successes with money? How have they changed how you deal with money?

Are there any other events or elements in your past that you think may be affecting your current relationship with money?

Now that we're at the end of these questions, take some time to check in with yourself. Is there anything important emerging for you, here? Any insights or curiosity bubbling up? Any lingering thoughts or images? How are you feeling?

I am so proud of you—you did great! Thinking about money with this level of intention, curiosity, and sustained focus is incredibly rare and no small feat. Well done, you!

Stop here for a moment. Take a deep breath and tune in to yourself. How do you feel after exploring your Money Story?

You might feel heavy, angry, excited, energized, grieving, overwhelmed, depleted, or some combination of these. Maybe you're feeling something else entirely. All of this is absolutely OK and normal. You are making progress in your money journey and growth looks different for everyone!

REFLECTION PAGE

With great love and respect, I want to gently urge you to take some time for self-care and integration.

A Body Check-In is a wonderful place to start.

Remember, the purpose of intentional integration is *not* to dwell on emotions or get stuck in the past. It's to help us honor what we have discovered and to digest and internally organize anything that may have been confusing, painful, or overwhelming for your younger self that has carried over for you now.

What would feel good to you to help you integrate the deep work you've done here? *A long walk in nature? A cuddle pile with your kittens? A cuppa tea with a trusted friend? You may find it fruitful to bring your money material into creative expression—like dance, drawing, painting, sculpture, music, writing, or poetry.*

As always, do what feels nourishing to you in the moment, and treat yourself with tender loving care and compassion.

VALUE/SELF-WORTH

For most people, value is intimately intertwined with money. Many of our struggles with money are, at heart, part of a quest to find, feel, and claim our self-worth.

Value has nothing to do with money and everything to do with money. Almost everyone has questions about the value they bring to money work.

On the one hand, it has nothing whatsoever to do with that number on your paycheck or bank statement. Value isn't something you *earn*; it's something you *are*. This is why we could never, ever put a number on your value. The idea that your value could be tallied or quantified is absurd. Your salary would need zeros to infinity.

Yet, intrinsic as our value is, we also need to find ways to monetize and quantify it in today's society. We need to earn a sustainable income and price our products and services in ways that feel good.

These function as strictly external mirrors of our inner sense of value. However, in my experience, we need to start with the internal, emotional work of growing our personal sense of value. Only then will external practices like negotiating a higher salary bear fruit.

Under-earning is one of the clearest symptoms of not feeling and claiming your value—and this is based on so much more than your income alone. You can have millions of dollars in the bank, yet exhaust yourself at work every week and take on others' problems because you just can't say no. That is undervaluing yourself. On the other hand, you might earn under $20K per year, live within your means according to your values and desires, and lead a joyful, satisfying life. I wouldn't call that undervaluing or under-earning.

Under-earning can be about underselling, under-expressing, under-loving. Or it could be over-giving, under-receiving—under-no-ing and over-yes-ing. It has everything to do with your experience of self-worth—whether or not this is reflected in your salary or job description.

Finding and claiming your value is a lifelong process of growth. It unfolds over time, in brave leaps and baby steps. It demands both internal and external work.

My experience of self-worth and value, and the ways they impact each other, has been one of constant discovery. Some lessons have repeated themselves enough times that I believe you'll find them useful as well.

TEN LESSONS LEARNED ON A PATH TO SELF-WORTH (ON THE INSIDE) AND INCREASED EARNING (ON THE OUTSIDE)

1. **Boundaries, boundaries, and more boundaries.** Oh, how I have come to love and depend on compassionate boundaries. So much, in fact, that I'm going to devote an entire section to my love of boundaries. Stay tuned. You need to stand by your noes to live your yeses fully.

2. Many years ago, I found myself in a painful loop of comparison and self-judgment. Once I recognized it, I often caught myself repeating this accidental mantra to myself, if you will: **"My job is to be myself. Nothing more, nothing less."** It was potent and so healing for me as I worked through those money patterns and emotions.

3. Get real with who you are and who you're not. Know what you're exceptional at—and what you suck at. **Don't do the things you suck at.** There's no need to pretend.

4. When I was invited to my first public speaking gig, I started hyperventilating. I was terrified. In the months leading up to the talk, I got to witness a barrage of negative self-talk (*"I'm not smart, I'm not articulate, I have nothing to say . . ."*). I saw them, deleted them, and replaced them. (*"I am smart, I am articulate, my voice needs to be heard . . ."*) I rocked the talk and never looked back. **Delete and replace the negative thought patterns that aren't serving you.**

5. Focus on your successes. Every single baby step you take is victory. **Celebrate everything.** This is how huge change happens.

6. **Find gratitude** in all the corners of your life. Focus on the good. Seek it out. Notice it. Appreciate it.

7. **Milk your mistakes or so-called failures.** Mistakes are ripe learning opportunities not to be ignored. Get back on track with more clarity and compassion.

8. **Fill your cup.** Lavish yourself with self-care, hikes, meditation, dancing, friends, and community. Many of these gifts cost nothing and give so much.

9. Author Barbara Stanny says that the number one prerequisite for change is to **"Be willing to be uncomfortable."** Making more money is the willingness to be uncomfortable. I would add that we feel uncomfortable when we're shifting any pattern. It's a good sign. Be open to stretching.

10. **Love yourself.** And then love yourself more, deeper, and better. 'Nuff said.

JOURNAL PROMPTS

Now it's your turn:

What does knowing your value mean to you?

Where in your life do you not claim your value?

Are there times when you feel solid and confident in your value, and other times when you are downright mean and devaluing yourself? When/how/why does this shift for you?

What holds you back from claiming your value? Do you have a perfectionist of an inner critic living inside your head? What do they say?

Do you have a money ceiling? What is the highest amount you've earned on an hourly/yearly basis? Notice it. Name it. Un-shame this.

How can you claim your value more in your day-to-day life? (Does this look like reassessing your prices? Reclaiming some free time? Negotiating a raise in your hourly rate? Seeking a promotion—or a job that is a better fit for who, and where, you are now?)

On a daily basis, what can you do to grow, cultivate, and claim your value, more and more? Give yourself permission to take baby steps here if it gets uncomfortable.

5

Adding New Chapters
to Your Money Story

Ripping out the early pages of our Money Story doesn't help anyone. It's by rereading these old stories, unraveling these old patterns, and honoring these young voices within us that we can integrate and eventually write new chapters.

You are always growing, evolving, learning, and changing. And your relationship with money is evolving right along with you—*especially* if you're consciously working on it.

Maybe your family of origin had a deep scarcity mentality when it came to money, and you carried that with you for years. But now that you're a successful entrepreneur in your forties, you have an easier time feeling confident and thriving in your financial world.

Or maybe you spent most of your life avoiding money or having other people take care of it for you—your parents, your spouse, your accountant—but you've started getting in touch with money in the past few years.

You're doing deep work here. It's time to update your financial identity from someone who avoids money to making brave steps toward friendship and being savvy with it.

We have the power to write new chapters in our Money Story anytime we like.

Here we can look back at painful old passages and reframe them or claim gifts buried deep within them. We can zoom out and put what our parents did with money into the wider lens of their own upbringing, challenges, lineage—and gifts, too.

Writing new chapters in our Money Story usually involves completing old ones—seeing them as we've just been doing, learning from them, and intentionally letting them go with ritual.

There is beauty in this release. With a little guidance, we can honor the old parts of our Money Story and gather their wisdom, while gently, and cleanly, cutting ties. The process of sifting through your Money Story and releasing the pieces that no longer serve you is important, challenging, and beautiful.

We cannot truly heal a wound without forgiveness.

There are always two sides to forgiveness—
the letting go and the moving forward.
We let go of old beliefs about money and choose
what new beliefs we want to carry into the future.

JOURNAL PROMPTS

Go to the Money Story section you filled out in chapter 4, and read through it again.

....

What teachings are you glad to have received? What would you like to keep?

Review what wasn't so helpful. What stories could use reframing or updating?

Take a moment to reflect. What would you *like* your new Money Story to include? Use this space to explore what that might look and feel like.

Review and look for all the ways, even the smallest ones, that you can reinforce your new Money Story in your journal.

MONEY HEALING RITUALS

Life is a ritual of love
Life is a ritual of union, and
Life is a dance of the divine.
—VISHWAS CHAVAN

I love ritual. I especially love those rituals we create ourselves for our own healing. And I extra-specially love those rituals we create ourselves for *Money* Healing!

Ritual is a tool that can help you change the energy, intention, and relationship to something that needs shifting. As you explore your personal Money Story and begin consciously crafting your relationship with money, ritual helps you take the insights and desires that bubble up and integrate them into your life.

Money Healing rituals are one of my favorite ways to *love yourself into transformation,* rather than shaming or yelling yourself into change.

For some of you, this idea of ritual may seem silly. You might wonder how significant or productive it could really be. Perhaps the concept is overwhelming, and you wouldn't know where to start, even though the concept piques your curiosity.

If you hear a whisper that there's something for you here, I encourage you to listen, experiment, and read on. And, if you are someone that swoons at the thought or smell of ritual, you're in the perfect place.

The beautiful thing is, ritual can be incredibly simple, accessible, meaningful, and seriously productive. In this context, a ritual is simply a ceremony used to mark change.

Transition, metaphorical or literal death and birth, initiation—any momentous change is a powerful invitation into healing ritual. When you create and craft your own, the sky's the limit. It can look, taste, and feel however you want it to. It is yours.

I first stumbled upon ritual early in my twenties when I was grieving the loss of a boyfriend, a deep love of mine who took his life at a very young age. As I sought healing, I found myself awake late into the night, blasting music and dancing by candlelight. I felt a profound knowing, an awareness from the deepest place, that I needed to ritualize myself toward wholeness and dance myself back into life again. Without realizing exactly what I was doing, I created an altar of mementos and the space to express myself and heal.

Through my personal journey and years of professional work, ritual has proven to be a gateway to healing, growth, and celebration. Here we find support to travel the liminal spaces and forge a bridge between the story we have lived and the new chapters we're inspired to write.

In the context of my money work, I consider ritual a crucial ingredient in the Money Healing phase. Here we delve deeply into the emotional, historical, and psychological territory of our money relationship. We move through our money shame, giving it a seat next to us—or a back seat, perhaps. We listen and apply massive doses of forgiveness, love, and compassion. The goal is to offer understanding and healing to our Money Story so that we are able to love ourselves toward change and move into some of the more practical aspects of money work.

A money ritual can be as simple as throwing a party to celebrate with all your friends when you pay off your car or student loan. It can be intimately personal, steeped in significance and meaning, joyfully lighthearted and playful, quietly still, or anything in between. Maybe you want to take time to prepare for your rituals, luxuriating in a decadent bath and dressing in your very best before you begin. Perhaps you would like to choose a song or reading to help you step into this sacred space.

The rituals we choose for ourselves are profoundly powerful. One member of the Art of Money community shared that they begin their own rituals with a Body Check-In to ground themselves as they get started. Then they address any challenging emotions or resistance they noticed during the check-in as if it were a small child. Greeting that shame, anxiety, or mental block, they thank it, and gently remind difficult feelings that it is safe to do this work. And they make a point of closing every ritual with a reward or celebration to honor the work.

This practice is for you, so steep your favorite soothing tea, light a fragrant candle, and bring your crystals, drum, or dancing shoes. Put on music that makes you feel grounded and connected, then curl up with your journal and favorite pen to write a letter to your old friend, money. What do you want to say? How do you want to feel? Set yourself free to create a sacred practice that belongs to you.

I encourage all of my students to consider creating a healing ritual to ease, expedite, and deepen this process—it is truly one of the most potent tools in our Money Healing journey!

And now that we've set the scene, allow me to cheerlead you through just that.

Forgiveness and completion are the most powerful goals we can ritualize in our Money Healing journey. They support us in releasing the past, honoring the completion of one chapter of our lives, allowing the shedding of old layers, and stepping fully into the next chapter.

FORGIVE. COMPLETE. RELEASE. LET GO.

Forgive yourself, forgive your parents, forgive your ancestors
    for what they did and didn't do.
Grieve what you never had and what you wish you'd never had.
    Let go of the anger, hurt, regret, shame, and stuck-ness.
End the cycle. Complete the chapter.
Bless it, thank it, and let it go.

No act of forgiveness is too small if it liberates you even a tiny bit.

Forgiveness Ritual/The Gift of Forgiveness

Ritual calls us to come with an attitude of gentle, compassionate curiosity—this doesn't need to be overly serious unless that feels right to you. Consider the main chapters, big events, important people, and emotionally significant experiences of your financial life, as we just explored them. Use the following questions to start creating your list of people and events you want to forgive and let go.

Who or what are you angry with or resentful toward? How long have you felt this way toward them?

What resentments or grievances are you holding against yourself? How long have you felt this way?

What, or who, do you feel ready to forgive?

Have compassion for your past decisions and behaviors. After all, what's the point in trying to update your financial life if you are very aggressive and critical of yourself the whole time?

If you're not ready to forgive someone (or yourself), why not?

It might take some time for you to find your rhythm with these questions. As you progress through them, you may find yourself building momentum. You may also find yourself realizing or remembering additional pieces to forgive over the coming days or weeks ahead. Remember, this is a process. Go at your own pace. Be patient. Be gentle.

Completion Ritual/The Gift of Completion
Start where you are. Take this opportunity to identify any beliefs around money you're ready to release now. Thank each one for the ways it has served you or kept you safe in the past . . . and let it go. If it feels good to you, identify a new, more supportive belief to take its place.

> When we release our old, stagnant beliefs
> about money, we have room in our hearts to create
> happier, healthier beliefs of our choosing.

OLD BELIEF, NEW BELIEF, NEXT BABY STEP

OLD BELIEF	NEW BELIEF	NEXT BABY STEP (IF NEEDED)

As you make progress releasing old beliefs, you may find that more and more ideas come bounding into your awareness. It might happen as soon as you start listing things or it may take more time to process. There is no rush, no need to hurry; you can revisit this list whenever you feel moved to.

Your timing is the only "right" timing here.

Take a deep breath.

You are exactly where you need to be.

Celebration.

Too often, we jump from one accomplishment into the next challenge without taking a breath in between. We need to make time to celebrate our successes so that we can integrate them and appreciate the goodness in our lives. Celebration is invigorating; it reinspires and propels us forward.

Take a few moments now to look back over your *Art of Money Workbook* progress so far.

The biggest shifts are often quiet, subtle, internal: Deeper self-trust and compassion. Finally forgiving our parents and letting go of old hurts and resentments. Claiming our value. Feeling more at home and at peace with our bodies and our lives.

What have you accomplished in your money relationship? What inner, emotional shifts or insights have you had? What external, practical steps have you taken?

What shifts have occurred, big or small? What clarity, healing, peace, or intimacy have you experienced? Where have you gotten brave and done, or said, or tried?

This money journey is ongoing—so we must celebrate every success along the way.

CELEBRATE EVERY VICTORY

No matter how small or subtle or insignificant it may appear . . . there is so much value in celebrating!

1.

2.

3.

4.

5.

CELEBRATE EVERY VICTORY

6.

7.

8.

9.

10.

WHAT ELSE CAN YOU CELEBRATE?

Come on, I bet you can think of more!

How can you celebrate? There are so many possible ways, and some of them you are already doing without calling them a "ritual." Where do you turn when you want to savor a good event in your life: A decadent bubble bath or glass of fine wine? Treating yourself to a special dinner or a night out with friends? A dance party in the living room? A quiet evening all to yourself? Escaping for a hike in nature? Something else? Brainstorm how you can celebrate in teeny, tiny ways and also in bigger ways, and begin to practice celebrating often. List your ideas here:

1.

2.

3.

4.

5.

Baby steps are beautiful. Small incremental shifts over time create huge transformation. The slower, gentler path often takes us deeper and eventually further.

**Welcome, dear Money Adventurer, to the second phase
of our journey together.**

Here we will cross the bridge from the deep emotional work of Money
Healing into the nuts and bolts of Money Practices.

Let's enter the land of numbers and systems to claim our tools.

Let's build a sustainable framework to hang our goals and aspirations on.

Let's learn the language of money and empower ourselves to get the
help we need.

Let's find resources to forge the path ahead and align ourselves with our
deepest values.

Let's build a bridge of healthy, meaningful habits to our future.

PHASE TWO

MONEY PRACTICES

6

Money as a Self-Care Practice

Money Practice, *n.*

Old definition: A horribly stressful, terrifically tedious something that I should do, even though I hate everything about it.

New definition: Everything I do, on an ongoing basis, to help bring more clarity, peace of mind, and success to my money relationship.

Constantly evolving, uniquely mine, and deeply nourishing. In this space, I find continual feedback that refines my self-awareness and how aligned I am with my values and intentions. I seek the very best support for my Money Practice that I can, and, in turn, it supports me—enhancing every moment and every area of my life.

SO . . . WHAT EXACTLY IS A SELF-CARE PRACTICE?

In my beautiful mountain town of Boulder, Colorado, people use the word *practice* surprisingly often. Here in the "Boulder Bubble," as we affectionately refer to it, people talk about all sorts: a meditation practice, a yoga practice, a healthy eating practice, a conscious sex practice, a gardening practice, a journaling practice, or an authentic communication practice.

While this might sound a little precious, it points to an important truth: we can take any area or habit in our lives, fill it with intention, awareness, and compassionate discipline, and reap profound rewards.

Self-care practices aren't just another to-do list of chores: they are essential for keeping us happy, sane, and growing. When we take the time to love and replenish ourselves, we reconnect with our true nature and return to the world more capable of sharing our gifts.

For me, self-care looks like a soothing lavender salt bath or a hike up my favorite mountain trail. For you, it might be dancing with friends, a massage, or belting karaoke at the top of your lungs. Maybe it's something else entirely. Chances are, though, it doesn't look like hanging out with a calculator and a bookkeeping program.

But what if you could turn your "money stuff" into a decadent self-care practice? What if it could feel every bit as luxurious as that bubble bath or whatever your version of that is? What if you actually looked forward to your Money Practice because it made you feel so much happier, more alive, and mindful? What if it could be founded on and reinforce your most cherished values? What if it connected you ever more deeply to yourself, the world around you, and even your spirituality—whatever that means to you?

All of this is truly possible when we approach our interactions with money as a self-care practice. So let's figure out exactly what that means.

A self-care practice is something you do consciously, with intention, on a regular basis, to support and grow yourself. It's a healthy habit that, over time, provides a cumulative benefit.

Every self-care practice I know of contains some version of the following three key ingredients.

First of all, a practice is something you do over and over again—and, ideally, get better at over time.

Second, every self-care practice is supportive and nurturing in some way. The benefits may be physical, emotional, mental, spiritual, or some combination thereof.

A regular Money Practice will do wonders for your financial world. By tracking your income, spending, and savings, you can wield more conscious control over this area of your life and align it ever more closely with your values. This level of work enables us to create a sacred space for self-care, steeped in beauty, comfort, and joy.

Here you decide what qualities you want to infuse into your life and your use of money. Here you connect more authentically with yourself *and* your aspirations. The benefits don't stop there, either. Regularly engaging with your money can also bolster your self-esteem, deepen your sense of safety, and strengthen your intimate relationships.

The best self-care practices connect us ever more deeply to ourselves, to each other, and to our spirituality. This is largely due to the repetitive nature of personal practices.

If you do the same Money Practice over and over again, it will come to reflect how you have grown and changed over time. You may understand yourself better, and more fully, and show up to your relationships with more peace of mind and playfulness.

Like any great self-care practice, your Money Practice can be a training ground where you deepen your emotional honesty, mindfulness, and compassion—for yourself and others. A successful Money Practice is a challenge you engage with consistently. It nurtures your finances, and much more than that, it connects you ever more deeply with yourself, others, and the world around you.

As important as what a Money Practice is, *how* we practice is perhaps even more significant.

JOURNAL PROMPTS

Take a moment here to reflect:

How do you currently engage with your money? Do you have a regular practice of reviewing your numbers?

When you think of self-care, what comes to mind? What are the ways you care for yourself now? How would you like to care for yourself?

What if you began to think of engaging with your money as a self-care practice? What might that look and feel like?

7

What Is a Money Date?

A Money Date is simply creating time and space for you to connect with your money and your relationship to it—and it's the core of your Money Practice.

Here we build healthy habits to get more honest, clear, and empowered.

This sort of date might not seem as exciting as other dates at first. But it is more fun than "Making My Budget," or "Paying the F—ing Bills," or "Keeping My Head in the Sand."

Money Dates can be gentle, sacred, playful, minimalist, or expansive; solo or with your honey, business partner, or friend; quick or luxuriously long. Any time you set aside to look at your money relationship and your money itself could be called a "Money Date."

This is the regular, ongoing practice that breathes life into a money relationship. *Money Dates change everything,* trust me.

There are three possible levels to a Money Date. You can integrate all of them into every date or focus on one at a time. You get to decide what is appropriate, what you're ready for, and what makes you feel comfortable and cared for—this is your practice and your journey.

1. **The Practical Level**—where we take action. This is the realm of bookkeeping and bills: taking a frank look at your real numbers, reconciling receipts and tracking your spending and income, taking stock and making phone calls to banks, your insurance company, and so forth.

2. **The Emotional-Psychological Level**—where we feel, name, and shift our money emotions. When we explore and redefine all our money beliefs, patterns, and dynamics, we are operating on this level.

3. **The Spiritual Level**—where we explore the idea that money carries our deeper values. Here we delve into what our money means in relation to trust, generosity, thriving, gratitude, and celebration.

To enjoy a healthy and fulfilling relationship with money, we really need to incorporate regular practices from each level. If we only focus on practical matters, we may find ourselves held hostage by emotional resistance or unconscious patterns. If we only focus on our spiritual insights, we may find ourselves in deep financial trouble. A robust Money Practice attends to each of the three levels, shifting and growing along with you on your journey.

GETTING STARTED WITH A MONEY PRACTICE— THE WEEKLY MONEY DATE

I recommend Money Dates on a daily, weekly, monthly, and annual basis. But for the purposes of this workbook, we're going to focus on the weekly money date. This exercise is the perfect starting point to become more intimate with your money.

When we have a Money Date, it's important to know that the *how* matters just as much as the *what*.

Remember: your Money Practice is all about empowerment, awareness, and enjoyment.
There is absolutely no need for being heavy or serious, let alone feeling guilty, overwhelmed, or self-critical.

So, whatever you do, make patience and gentleness your closest companions along this journey. Engage with your Money Practices in a way that feels like taking exquisitely good care of yourself. Infuse them with your personality and preferences to make them your own.

Let's start by dipping our toes into the *what* of your weekly money date. A weekly Money Date doesn't have to be arduous or overly long—there's a lot you can get done in just twenty to thirty minutes, or even an hour if you wish. As with all Money Practices, consistency is key. So set your intention, make it doable, and get to it!

TWENTY-SEVEN WAYS TO MAKE A MONEY DATE YOUR OWN

1. **Light a candle to open the space as you start.** Blow the candle out when you've finished your Money Date to bring your time to an end.

2. **Play some favorite music** to get you in the mood. Try something that makes you feel like your best self.

3. **Clear off your desk to create a clean, calm space.** A clean desk can help clear the mind.

4. **Start with an intention.** Articulate what your hopes and priorities are for this time. "For the next hour, I want to be truly kind to myself. Whenever I catch myself getting anxious, I want to remember that I'm learning, and it's OK that I don't know everything. I am proud of myself for showing up."

5. **Attend to financial to-dos.** Enter and file any receipts that remain from the week. Check your numbers in your tracking system. Review your account balances and transactions online, making sure nothing seems unusual or out of place. Pay bills. Transfer money between accounts.

6. **Upgrade your bookkeeping system.** I can't tell you how many people are still using a spreadsheet someone made them years ago

that they *can't stand*. Give yourself an upgrade! Spend a little time investigating Mint, YNAB, MoneyGrit., Quicken, QuickBooks, and other tracking systems until you find one that feels good enough for you to learn.

7. **Speaking of learning a bookkeeping system**—do it! Don't just download it and then expect that you'll magically know how to use it. Spend a little time with a video tutorial or hire a bookkeeping trainer to show you the ropes.

8. **Reconsider your spending categories.** Maybe you want a whole "self-care" category for acupuncture, massage, and your gym membership. Or perhaps you're craving more connection and want to set aside funds for dinners and movies out with friends.

9. **Decide how you want to show up in a money-related conversation.** Even if you're calling your credit card company to dispute a charge, you can decide to be a warm, friendly voice on the other end of the line—or even strive to make them laugh!

10. **Move your body!** Take a dance break when you start feeling stiff and restless or do some gentle yoga or qigong before you start.

11. **Nibble homeopathic doses of dark chocolate.** Or indulge in whatever delectable treat appeals most to you!

12. **Invite a friend.** You might meet at a coffee shop, catch up for a few minutes, then each work on money stuff for an hour, and debrief afterward. Choose a very trusted friend!

13. **Listen to something money-related** to inspire you before you begin. *Ahem, did you know I have a whole podcast? Go to baritessler.com to listen in!*

14. **Clean up a "money leak."** Are you still paying for an old gym membership or Hulu account you're not using?

15. **Consider your financial support team** (bookkeepers, accountants, financial planners, financial therapists, etc.). Who is on your team? Is it time to add or swap out a member?

16. **Check in with your values.** It's important to know your values *and* how they change. What's more important to you now than a year ago—so much so that you're willing to spend a bit more on it? Maybe you need more self-care right now or the house needs repairs before you can sell it. Listen. Notice.

17. **Check in on the money areas** of spending, earning, saving, debt repayment, and investing. What area do you want to focus on and learn about right now? You don't have to tackle all of them at once!

18. **Celebrate your strengths.** What are you *great at* when it comes to money? We're hardwired to focus on negative things, but choosing to name positive things instead reinforces them! Name your successes. From modest to monumental, they are all part of your journey and worthy of recognition and celebration.

19. **Do a Body Check-In.** This foundational practice will help you connect better with yourself while making room for all of your emotions—tough ones and terrific ones alike.

20. At least once during your Money Date, **do another Body Check-In.** (YES! I'm repeating this! It's that important!) Notice what you're feeling in your body, emotions, and thoughts. Just observe with compassionate curiosity. Deep breath. Pause. *Annnnnnd* continue on.

21. **Check in with your generosity.** If you could be contributing generously to any cause or group right now, what would that be? Would you like to set that up? Are you already contributing, but it feels like an uncomfortable stretch and you want to pull back or hit pause for a bit? Are there other, nonmonetary ways you'd like to express your generosity?

22. **Make a list of ten** (or fewer) things you'd like to fine-tune or improve in your money relationship over the next six months. Maybe you want to learn a bookkeeping program, take an evening to explore some childhood money memories, or think about your business expenses differently. I am always tweaking my Money Practices; we're never "done" with money, and that's OK!

23. **Identify the spending habits *you* want to shift.** This isn't one size fits all! For example, some of my Art of Money students are surprised to notice how much they deprive themselves and over-think and find that indulging themselves a bit more feels really empowering! It can take some time, but get curious and start to notice what *your* patterns are. They might not be the same as everyone else's.

24. **Reframe a "mistake."** So many of our liabilities are actually hidden assets when we learn to see them in a fresh way. Did you learn a big lesson from a "mistake" or have an amazing, life-changing adventure thanks to that debt you're paying off? Consider how you can shift your perspective to find the positive in those experiences.

25. **What can you *celebrate* right now about your money relationship?** This is so important, and I know you can find things if you look. Make a list of ten things to celebrate, and yes, simply having a Money Date is a huge cause for celebration.

26. **Dedicate time to your *Art of Money Workbook.*** This might look like continuing your work through the practices and exercises shared here. Or perhaps it could be rereading a section that feels deeply meaningful and then sitting with how it speaks to you—and how that feels.

27. **Close with a prayer of gratitude or something meaningful to you,** like the loving-kindness meditation: "May all beings be healthy. May all beings be happy. May all beings be free from suffering. May all beings be at peace."

Remember: every time you interact with money
is an opportunity to grow into more self-awareness,
compassion, and empowerment.

Let's start exploring how you can make your Money Dates personally meaningful and significant for you.

Where will you do your weekly Money Practice? Make literal room for this budding new practice and relationship.

What do you want this space to feel like? What qualities, mood, or energy will support you in your Money Practices? E.g.: Does calm simplicity help you relax and focus? Does lush beauty reassure you? How about comfort, playfulness, sacredness, relaxation, commitment, or clarity? Write out the qualities that come to mind for you.

How can you decorate your space or arrange things to bring out these qualities? What elements or objects might support these feelings for you?

MAKING IT HAPPEN:
THREE MONTHS OF MONEY DATES

Use these questions to help guide and inspire you as you build your personal practice.

What are you going to do during your Money Date this week?

When are you going to do it? Put your Money Date on the calendar! Who says you can't schedule it—and even look forward to it?

What tools or supplies do you need on your Money Date to feel better supported?

How are you going to make it feel creative, joyful, luxurious, and pleasurable?

Follow-up: How did it go? What did you end up doing during your Money Date?

How long did you devote to your Money Date?

What did you learn?

What can you do to make it better and/or more fun next time?

There's always a learning curve when starting
a Money Practice. Please don't beat yourself up
for not knowing how to do everything perfectly
on day one or even one hundred and one.

MONEY PRACTICE REFLECTION PAGE

How many times have you done your weekly practice this month?

What challenges have you faced? What is there to celebrate?

What's supported your consistency and success? What's gotten in your way?

What feelings have come up during the week around your daily practices or money in general?

Is there something you'd like to shift or adjust in your weekly practice? What can you do to make it better—more effective, impactful, authentic, or fun?

What are you learning about your relationship with money from your Money Dates?

Don't forget to celebrate and appreciate yourself for engaging with your Money Practice.

Honor the fact that you're here, showing up.

Committing time and space for your Money Practice is truly such a profound and loving act for yourself and your whole life. Take a moment to really feel some gratitude for yourself, along with any people or factors in your life that have supported you in following through on this commitment.

Dark chocolate for everyone! Or, you know, whatever tastes like celebration to you.

BODY CHECK-INS

Exercise #1: Before Money Interaction

I felt . . .

My thoughts, intuitions, realizations . . .

Exercise #2: During Money Interaction

I felt . . .

My thoughts, intuitions, realizations . . .

Exercise #3: After Money Interaction

I felt . . .

My thoughts, intuitions, realizations . . .

8

Welcome to
Values-Based Bookkeeping

So we've talked about Money Practices and started to embrace these on a weekly basis. But it's pretty hard to maintain your Money Practices if you don't have some kind of system to track your numbers and know where you stand.

That's all a bookkeeping system is, folks! It's simply a way to keep on top of your earnings, spending, and savings. It really is that simple— even if it doesn't feel like it, yet. We'll get there.

To track your numbers, you will need to choose a bookkeeping system and learn how to use it. This is nonnegotiable.

I cover this in greater detail in my book and yearlong money course *The Art of Money*, but I'll give you the basics here as well. Rest assured that there is no perfect or right bookkeeping program, you just need to find one you're actually comfortable using.

Here are a few examples of bookkeeping programs you might choose from: Mint, YNAB, MoneyMinder, Quicken (personal), QuickBooks and Wave (business), Excel, and Numbers.

I see so many people get hung up on choosing a system. In fact, I've been there myself.

There are so many options available that we get overwhelmed trying to pick "the perfect one." We get stuck weighing the pros, cons, and features of different systems. We also make the mistake of thinking that whichever one we choose, we have to stick with it for life. We tense up. We forget to make it fun and playful, creative and meaningful!

I'm here today to tell you: Just pick one. Then start using it. Baby steps. You can do this!

It can take time to learn a bookkeeping system—sometimes months.

Give yourself three to six months of weekly Money Dates, and then ease yourself into bookkeeping with that extra loving awareness that you've started to cultivate in your relationship to money.

If you decide to use a bookkeeping program, don't just download it—spend some time actually learning how to use it. Some systems are simpler than others, and you can learn the ropes on your own—or watch their video tutorials (like Mint and YNAB). But many of us need a good bookkeeping trainer (*yes*, these angels exist!), especially if we're learning QuickBooks, MoneyGrit, or Quicken. That's totally fine! Getting support is *such* a good thing—so celebrate it!

This is a gentle reminder to go at your own pace. Give yourself permission to get the support you need. Shower yourself with patience and compassion—this takes courage. Don't let that hold you back, though, because this work can also be profoundly empowering! You're learning. Honor the journey by giving yourself grace and lots of loving encouragement.

> There is no such thing as picking the wrong bookkeeping system. Take the pressure off and give yourself permission to experiment. You are allowed to shift your tools and practices over time.

Consider this a loving little fire lit beneath you. You really can do this! No matter how good or bad at math you were. No matter how long it's been. Whether you had a system in place and let it fall by the wayside, and now you're ready to start again. Or even if you've never given bookkeeping a try.

VALUES-BASED BOOKKEEPING

While I can't teach you how to use a bookkeeping system in this work-book, I can show you how to make your bookkeeping a lot more playful, creative, and meaningful.

If you think bookkeeping is oh-so-dry, dusty, and dull that even just thinking of a spreadsheet puts you to sleep, this approach is for you.

One of the simplest, most profound, and playful ways I've found to bring our values into our money relationship is by renaming the categories within our bookkeeping system. If you don't have a tracking system yet, don't worry about it! You can still do this exercise to prepare for when you have one in place.

> If you want to successfully create a satisfying
> relationship with your bookkeeping system,
> you must connect it with your personal values.

Money is always, always intertwined with our values, and if we don't honor that, our enthusiasm wanes dramatically. No one benefits from that, so it's time to take a new approach. If you have even the slightest hint of resistance about beginning a bookkeeping practice, this concept of renaming might just have you singing a much happier tune.

It's time to have some fun! You might start by looking at your expenses and asking yourself if you could find a more meaningful or playful name for any of them. For example, you might not consider "Rent" one of your personal *values*, but when you frame it as "My Personal Sanctuary" on your expenses, you might just realize how central it is to you.

Or you could look at your values list first, and see what expenses already fit under them. "Community" is a core value, so do your travel, phone, internet, and dinner parties with friends belong there?

You don't need to rename everything. But be sure to try on—at least as a thought exercise—what it would feel like if you saw "Love Shack" in your monthly bookkeeping record instead of "Mortgage."

Your expenses are the primary place to use values-based bookkeeping, but feel free to play with this in other money areas: your income, investing, savings, gifting, etc.

What really matters to me? What is most important? What feels beneficial and meaningful? You can list your values as single words or phrases—whatever feels right to you. Also consider values that aren't currently a part of your life that you would like to start prioritizing. What about self-care? Creativity? Family? Expansion? Generosity?

What do I value most at this phase in my life? List ten things or more.

1.

2.

3.

4.

5.

6.

7.

8.

9.

10.

What are your monthly expenses? Depending on how much time, energy, and money you have, you may go through several months' worth of bank statements for these numbers, or you might make some estimates to get started.

Hand on heart, how do your soul-based values and reality-based expenses line up?

Get clear on your values. Track how much time/energy/money you really spend on them. And take action to bring them to life. What spending, saving, or income categories in your money tracking system could you rename, reimagine, or reframe to reflect these values?

Looking for a little inspiration? Take a peek at Imagining Your Values-Based Expense Chart before you get started.

IMAGINING YOUR VALUES-BASED EXPENSE CHART

EXPENSES	ALTERNATE NAME	BACK UP OPTIONS
AUTO	Hot Wheels	Pathfinder, Trusty Steed, Locomotion
Auto Insurance	Peace of Mind	Safety Hatch, Back-Up Plan, Escape Route
Car Loan/Payment	Auto-mony	Motor-vation, Move Freely, Go Where the Wind Calls
Gas	Hit the Road	Wind at My Back, Keep the Motor Running, Wheels Keep Turning
Maintenance & Repairs	Auto Update	Mech Check, Car Name Spa Day
License/Registration	Ticket to Ride	Vroom Degree, Scroll of Vroom, Movin' Papers, Ticket to Freedom
CONTRIBUTION	Paying It Forward	Community Building. Helping Hand, Conscious Community
Tax Deductible Contributions	Sharing the Way Forward	Growing Together, Gifts of Gratitude, Future Funding
Other Giving	Grateful Generosity	Community Shares, Gifts of the Heart, Share the Wealth, Generous Journey
CREATIVITY	Create Inspiration	Siren Song, Mind of the Muse, Artistic Expression, Choose Inspiration
Art Supplies	Artist's Toolbox	Prop Table, Tools of Creation, Artist's Lens, Visioning Tools
Art Classes	Creation Community	Inspired Learning, Art Haven, Roots of Art, Branching Out
Theater - Dance Classes	Self-Expression	Freedom to Groove, Express Yourself, Dance it Out, Act Out Loud, Bust a Move
FINANCIAL		
Retirement/Investment/ Long-Term Savings	Resilience Deposit	Legacy, Nest Egg, Safety Net, Cheers to the Future, Pave the Way
Bank Fees	Mindful Banking	System Access, Number Tracking
CC Finance Charges	Flexibility	Early Access, Room to Flex, Breathing Room, Back-up Plan
Loan Interest	Thankful Future	Degree of Gratitude, Future Fruit, Grateful to Grow, Choosing Forward

FUN & PLAY	Time to Frolic	Cut Loose, Get Connected, Frolic with Friends, Seek Joy, Choose Joy
Art & Culture	Art Is Life	Creative Perspective, Artistic Inspiration, My Muse, Life Is Art
Dining Out	Together at the Table	Nourish + Connect, Dine Connection, Tableside Togetherness
Movies	Cinematic Escape	Films n' Fun, Screen Escape, Adventures in Film, Family Films, Popcorn Party
Music/Concerts	Lost in the Music	Get Your Groove On, Shake Your Groove Thing, Musicality, Play That Tune
Recreation Equip	Fun-cessories	Ready to play, Playtime toolbox, Funtime toys, Funvestment, Future Fun Times
Recreations	Shenanigans	Fancy Free, Funtime, Free Play, Choose to Play, Play Party, Fun with Friends

Now, it's time to grab a cozy cup of tea, get comfy, and use the following chart to create categories that belong to *you*. Shimmy your shoulders and take a deep breath. Throw on some music that makes you feel *good* and give yourself permission to play!

Go wild! Make it feel uplifting and lighthearted. This is the fun part!

Feel free to start with a rough or incomplete draft and let it simmer in your head for a few days. Remember, nothing is written in stone here—you can revisit, shift, and adjust as needed!

Make a monthly Money Date of reviewing your categories and trying on different titles as you grow. Be creative, keep it light, and have fun!

Values-based bookkeeping is one powerful way to breathe life into your hopes and live your dreams day by day, one baby step at a time.

VALUE-BASED BOOKKEEPING

EXPENSE CATEGORY	VALUES-BASED NAME
AUTO	
Auto Insurance	
Car Loan/Payment	
Gas	
Maintenance & Repairs	
License/Registration	
CONTRIBUTION	
Tax Deductible Contributions	
Other Giving	
CREATIVITY	
Art Supplies	
Art Classes	
Theater - Dance Classes	
FINANCIAL	
Retirement/Investment/ Long-Term Savings	
Bank Fees	
CC Finance Charges	
Loan Interest	
FUN & PLAY	
Art & Culture	
Dining Out	
Movies	
Music/Concerts	
Recreation Equip	
Recreations	

9

Spiritual Money Practices

Now that we've covered the practical and emotional sides of our self-care-based Money Practices, I want to draw your attention to some spiritual practices you can incorporate into your daily, weekly, monthly, and yearly money relationship.

With mindfulness and heart, even paying your bills or reconciling your accounts can become an authentic mindfulness practice of bringing your fullest, most essential self into the world.

Over the years, I've come to rely on four fundamental practices to support this deeper level of money work: generosity, trust, thriving, and gratitude. Think of them as invitations to an intimate inquiry, ways to honor what is happening in your life, or simply interesting perspectives to consider and take to heart as you follow your money-and-life journey.

GENEROSITY

In many religious and spiritual traditions, generosity—and even regular giving—is encouraged. I think there is a beautiful teaching at the heart of all of these messages: we should be as generous as we can with our time, energy, and, yes, money.

That "as we can" part, though? It is crucial.

If your generosity toward others harms you, it is not truly generosity.

Do you have the resources to make financial contributions?

What are some nonmonetary ways you can show generosity: donating your time or services?

What type or style of contribution speaks to your soul? Is it gifts or donations? Get creative here.

Members of my Art of Money community practice generosity in eclectic ways, from offering a compassionate ear to a friend or chauffeuring the elderly to and from doctor's visits to making sandwiches and giving them to folks struggling with housing insecurity.

In a very real and tender way, the practice of generosity points us to the profound truth of our innate connection with others and the world we all share.

Self-awareness and self-compassion are essential elements of generosity.

Each of us needs to find our own balance in generosity, depending upon what our resources are at this particular point in our lives.

Be generous with others *and* yourself. You cannot pour from an empty cup. Make a point of checking in regularly with yourself, your finances, and your connection with your concept of what is greater than yourself.

TRUST

Many people find it incredibly challenging to trust themselves with money—just thinking about finances might make them feel deeply unsafe. They might mistrust their own ability to effect change, the financial institutions they interact with, or even the simple possibility that *everything will be OK*.

If you've invested some time and effort into Money Practices, you might notice yourself building your self-trust brick by brick. Yet you may also peel back layer after layer of beliefs and emotions, only to discover a deep foundation of mistrust.

I like to think of trust as an ingredient we can stir into our money work. Doing some practical money work or looking at your emotional stuff around money? Stir in some trust. If this seems challenging, take heart; you can actively work to cultivate trust.

Each time I go for a hike, I grow my trust. I tune in to my body and offer up my fear, anxiety, excitement, anger, and joy to the universe. You might experience and deepen your own sense of trust through gardening, playing with your grandchildren, watching the sunset, or volunteering at a soup kitchen. Some people practice meditation, prayer, or other devotional work to cultivate trust, while others delve into great works of philosophy. You might personally experience trust through dance or other movement practices.

Find whatever brings you a greater connection with yourself and a sense of faith-filled well-being. Know that cultivating trust is deeply relevant to your money work. It is part of the journey.

There is a rhythmic, cyclical nature to life and money. When we recognize this, we can relax into trust. We can *know*, with faith and certainty, that *everything* in life is temporary. Even the most challenging moments will pass.

Trust doesn't whitewash the pain or reality of challenging situations. It infuses them with grace, a little spaciousness, and ease so we can move through the difficult times.

JOURNAL PROMPTS

Check in with yourself. How do you feel, in your body and otherwise, when you think of the word *trust*?

Do you feel you have trust in yourself? In others? Why or why not?

What might it look like if you were able to trust yourself more? How might that feel in your body?

How might you begin to cultivate more trust? What practices could you add into your life?

THRIVING

Controversial confession time: I'm not a huge fan of the word *abundance*. Over the past twenty years or so, it has become a buzzword for anything having to do with money.

I prefer the word thriving *to describe that incredibly powerful and essential human experience marked by dignity, joy, and resilience.*

There are so many facets, levels, and subjective aspects to thriving—and, as always, they include the financial numbers, yet also go far beyond them.

A 2010 Princeton study found that emotional well-being for Americans increased along with income—but only up to a certain point. Once individuals earned $75,000 per year, continued income growth showed minimal or no benefit to their emotional well-being.

Of course, there are a multitude of factors at play here, from the varying costs of living in different areas to the number of our dependents, strength of our support networks, and on and on. **Few of us can thrive when we're worried about basic needs like food, shelter, health care, or surviving into old age. However, it's rarely that simple.**

Thriving looks different to everyone, and our perceptions and ability to experience it change over the course of our lives—sometimes independent of our financial reality!

Many people thrive in very **simple, low-income lives,** thanks to wonderful community connections, devotional religious practices, or fulfilling work. On the other hand, **I've known more than a few millionaires who struggled to take a single, satisfied breath.**

We all have our own pathways to thriving, including our practical, emotional, and spiritual pursuits.

As you continue your journey, you may discover that you truly need to increase your income, or start a "life happens" fund. (Isn't that a nicer name than "emergency fund"?) You might be able to utterly shift your sense of well-being, at least for a time, by splurging on a great meal or dancing alone in your kitchen. We can also deepen our capacity for thriving by **recognizing the gifts we already have,** living within our means, and **taking time to enjoy the small pleasures in life.**

Stop here for a moment to consider what thriving might look like in your life. Use the following prompts to guide you as you explore this money frontier further. If this exercise feels challenging to you, go slowly.

Take a deep breath. Do a Body Check-In. You are safe here.

Tune in to yourself and ask: What do *I* need to thrive?

Be open to the answers that come.

If you find yourself longing to thrive more, it's worth taking this inquiry seriously.

What do I need to thrive emotionally . . .?

What do I need to thrive mentally . . .?

What do I need to thrive physically . . .?

What are my personal gateways to greater thriving—however small or surprising?

What are the simple pleasures in life that bring me immense joy?

Think back on the last few weeks or months: What has brought a sense of thriving to you? What can you learn by reflecting on happy times and moments?

GRATITUDE

Ah, gratitude. It is so beautiful, so life-changing, and sometimes *so* challenging.

Life and money can feel—and *be*—so hard. Yet, even on our toughest days—perhaps *especially* on our toughest days—we can pause a few moments, take a few breaths, and shift our focus to gratitude.

Sometimes, we get so goal-focused that we lose sight of the beauty right in front of us. Or we achieve one milestone—like raising your credit score or paying off that debt—only to move directly to the next project. We keep chasing achievements without pausing to appreciate, celebrate, or rest.

No matter how much or how little you have in the bank, please— pause and feel into gratitude.

Take the time, take a moment, take a breath, and be grateful for all that you have, all that you've done, and all that you are.

List fifty things you're grateful for in your life. It might be that savings fund you worked so hard for—or it might simply be this moment, sipping a cozy cup of tea, listening to the robins chirp outside your window.

Dear Money Adventurer,

Our first big theme in this section is visioning. Now, you might find yourself wondering: What is visioning?

This is where we dive into your wildest dreams. Here we paint the big picture of your desiring. This is audacious imagining.

So how comfortable does that sound to you?

Here's the thing—you might think visioning sounds like the most fun thing ever, or maybe just reading about it makes your skin crawl a little.

There is no judgment here.

We all have our own strengths and growing edges. For some of you, this material will feel like home. You'll waltz effortlessly, gleefully among dreams, visions, and values.

For others, this is challenging territory—rough, unfamiliar terrain, shadowed and foreboding. Some of us were never encouraged to "dream big." Scarcity, responsibility, or social expectations overpowered our deepest desires and rewrote our priorities for us. It's difficult to even connect with big-picture dreams, let alone imagine bringing them to life.

Fear not.

Whether you love this stuff or find it challenging, there is value and meaning for you here. The only right pace is your pace, and some paths are more challenging than others—sometimes when we least expect it.

I'm here to hold your hand, every step of the way.

Be gentle with yourself.

We're diving deep.

Allow yourself to be surprised—it may be more challenging, playful, meaningful, sorrowful, or exciting than you think!

Here's to showing up. Here's to honoring your whole self.

Here's to making dreams come true.

MONEY MAPS

10

Visioning

Money can be your tool, your partner,
to create the life you envision for yourself.

Visioning is the term for using your mind's eye to imagine possibilities for the future. It's seeing what is not yet here, but *could* be. When I talk about the importance of vision and visioning in deep money work, I'm usually talking about your personal vision for yourself and your future, and maybe your family's vision as well. The following questions help us explore our heart's desires and connect with what we would like to see.

Before you start journaling through these questions, please know:

Like most things in life, visioning comes easily to some and less easily to others. You may already be well-practiced at visioning. Or you may have never done it—not even once. Here's some help to wade into the visioning process:

JOURNAL PROMPTS

What do you want? I mean deeply, truly, soul-level *desire* for your life?

What gives your life meaning and purpose?

What gets you excited about being alive?

What does a happy life look like for you right now when it comes to your finances? (It will be different for everyone.) *Is it earning more money, aggressively paying down debt and spending less . . . or is it working a little less? Are you achieving your financial goals by slashing expenses or by earning more? Perhaps both?*

Imagine yourself five to ten years down the line, with a comfortable amount of money. Just *beginning* to think about this can be powerful.

How would you live your life in this space?

What would be different from how you currently live your life?

What would you do with all that money?

Let yourself effortlessly imagine your way into the landscape. What else do you notice?

Imagine you only have twenty-four hours to live.

In this vision, instead of focusing on what you'd like to do with your final hours, it's time to reflect and look back at your life.

Ask yourself the following questions . . . and let their answers come without too much thought:

Which of your dreams for your life have come true?

Which dreams of yours didn't come true?

What got overlooked, unattended, or underappreciated in your life?

If your life were ending now, what would be left unfulfilled?

From the beautiful vision you've allowed to emerge, now it's time to create a pathway that takes you there. And that brings up an uncomfortable and possibly triggering topic.

Now, come back to your center.

Take as much time as you need to write. Honor everything that arose, no matter how small or large, soft or loud. Write whatever comes to you, in whatever form it comes.

~ 11 ~

Transform Budgeting with Money Maps

How does the word budget *make you feel?*

I don't know about you, but I can sense my jaw tighten and my tummy getting a little queasy just looking at that dreadful word.

Budget. Blech. I just don't like it—and I don't like a lot of what it stands for.

Yes, I'm saying this even as a financial therapist!

I know I'm not alone. Almost every person I've ever worked with has carried some level of "budget baggage." Can you relate?

Most people think about budgets as a restrictive regimen that harshly limits their spending.

"OK, only $50 per week on groceries—that's it!"

"No, I can't go to the movies with you, because it's not in my budget." Sad trombone.

Like a fiercely restrictive diet where you count calories and weigh out food portions, this kind of spending plan robs you of your freedom and joy. It reeks of disempowerment. It sets up a dynamic where the budget is your external authority figure, telling you what you can and cannot do.

This kind of rigidity naturally leads to rebellion.

That's why budgeting like this is almost always doomed to fail. Just as overly strict diets lead to guilt-ridden binges, overly strict budgets often lead to defiant overspending. Do you see how wise you are to resist budgeting, if you think it'll play out like this?

Thankfully, this budgeting approach is not at all what we're about here. Our focus is on empowerment and creativity and listening to your inner authority to align your life and money with your personal values and beliefs. That's what sets this approach to budgeting apart.

Here I'm going to introduce you to a new concept: creating your Money Map. A far cry from that boring old budget, your Money Map is born of your hopes and aspirations, weaving together what you values, dreams, and desires.

JOURNAL PROMPTS

Have you tried budgeting before and found it too restrictive?

What happened when you kept a budget? How did it feel?

Did that make you resist budgeting in the future?

How does it feel when you look at your numbers? How can you bring more ease and joy to budgeting now?

Ready to learn a new and exciting way to do this work?

It's way more fun than you probably expect, I promise.

CREATING YOUR THREE-TIER MONEY MAP

The next step in your journey is the creation of your Money Map (not *budget*, blech), which I like to teach in three tiers: *the Basic Needs Lifestyle Plan*, *the Comfortable Lifestyle Plan*, and *the Ultimate Lifestyle Plan*.

I encourage you to engage with all three tiers to get the fullest possible picture of where you are and the potential for where you want to go.

If, after starting with the Basic Needs Plan, you feel that you've got plenty to work with for now, that's fine. Or perhaps the Basic Needs and Comfortable Lifestyle Plans feel right for you, and that's totally OK, too.

Here, everyone gets to create their own personal definitions and parameters for each of the three tiers.

REFLECTIONS

Now, take some time to simply reflect on what each lifestyle means to you. This exercise will help you start to envision and define each of the three tiers. Write out your thoughts, feelings, and definitions for each one in the following sections.

Remember to take time for a Body Check-In as you explore each tier and honor the feelings that come up for you.

My Basic Needs Lifestyle

These are the bare-bones, bottom-line needs for your happy life. Is it just groceries, rent, and utilities? Does it include a gym membership? A certain type of food? Does it include savings? Is a daily latte a must?

You're the boss here.

My Comfortable Lifestyle

At this level, we introduce more comfort into your lifestyle. Does this look like a monthly massage or pedicure? Some disposable income for weekly meals out? Do you start traveling?

My Ultimate Lifestyle

Here we progress to the final tier. Imagine having sufficient income to live out the fullest expression of your soul's deepest desires and wildest dreams. What does that look like to you?

CALCULATING YOUR INCOME

Now let's go deeper and bring in some numbers.

Begin this step of the process by listing out your average monthly income for the coming year. Then, slowly and carefully list out each of your expenses to find your monthly average.

Some of you know your exact income. Either you have a salaried position or you are a well-established entrepreneur. Others may be business owners whose income fluctuates over the year. If you need to, use your best estimates.

Deep breath. We all have to start somewhere.

CALCULATING YOUR EXPENSES

Next, we move on to organizing your expenses. Begin by listing your bottom-line expenses, those expenses that are must-haves. These are nonnegotiable. I usually call them your "basic needs."

I want to emphasize that you are the only one who can decide what expenses belong here. For instance, some people feel that auto expenses belong to their basic needs because having a car is an essential part of their lives. Meanwhile, other folks are fine getting around on public transportation or riding their bike.

Years ago, I felt that eating organic food was critically important for me, so I placed that in my basic needs. Of course, many people never buy organic food even if they have plenty of money.

This is personal stuff, even if you've never thought of it that way before.

Along with this variability between people, there's also variability over time. Your decision about whether a certain expense item is a basic need might change as you continue your journey. That is a normal part of this. You're doing great.

Do your best to get exact numbers.

Dig out those bank statements and your credit card statements. If you don't know the exact number, or if the expense is variable over time, use your best estimate for now. For expenses that occur only a few times per year—like car maintenance—generate your best estimate, and divide that by twelve to find your monthly cost. Use the following chart to help keep yourself organized and track your progress.

This is a loving reminder that sometimes this work might feel heavy or trigger challenging emotions. Give yourself permission to take a break. Stretch. Walk away if you need to, and come back when you're ready.

This space is for you. This journey is yours. All of you is welcome here.

TIER ONE: BASIC NEEDS PLAN

EXPENSES	MONTHLY AVERAGES
Rent or Mortgage	
Home Repair	
Utilities	
Phone	
Internet	
Dining Out	
Groceries	
Car Expenses	
Health Insurance	
Entertainment	
Clothing	
Self-Care	
Gifts	
Education	
School Loans	
Travel	
Credit Card Payments	
Savings	
Taxes	
Investments	
Total Expenses	

Does your income meet your basic needs right now or not?

How do you feel about this?

Give yourself permission to be curious, and cut yourself some slack. This is about learning, not self-judgment. Notice it all with compassion and gentle curiosity.

Take the time here to observe what you feel as you look over your expenses, at the totals of each category, and, finally, your grand total.

To know and look squarely at your numbers is a *really big deal*. It's very courageous, mature, responsible, and rare! You did a brave thing here today.

Going through this process will take you a long way toward setting intentions around your money relationship for next year and turning those intentions into your reality!

Good luck, dear traveler! This is incredibly beautiful and important work you're doing! Take a deep breath, and trust the process. You've got this.

I know you do.

Now it is time to celebrate yet another big step you've taken and the progress you've made.

I'm proud of you.

Give yourself permission to be proud of yourself, too. Luxuriate in that feeling for a little while. Rest there, and allow yourself to bask in the glow of self-love and self-care.

TIER TWO: COMFORTABLE LIFESTYLE PLAN

EXPENSES	MONTHLY AVERAGES
Rent or Mortgage	
Home Repair	
Utilities	
Phone	
Internet	
Dining Out	
Groceries	
Car Expenses	
Health Insurance	
Entertainment	
Clothing	
Self-Care	
Gifts	
Education	
School Loans	
Travel	
Credit Card Payments	
Savings	
Taxes	
Investments	
Total Expenses	

TIER THREE: ULTIMATE LIFESTYLE PLAN

EXPENSES	MONTHLY AVERAGES
Rent or Mortgage	
Home Repair	
Utilities	
Phone	
Internet	
Dining Out	
Groceries	
Car Expenses	
Health Insurance	
Entertainment	
Clothing	
Self-Care	
Gifts	
Education	
School Loans	
Travel	
Credit Card Payments	
Savings	
Taxes	
Investments	
Total Expenses	

This three-tier framework is supportive and illuminating no matter what your income level or expenses are.

It helps to reorganize your relationship with your expenses, clarify the different levels of your lifestyle, and consciously bring yourself into alignment with the lifestyle that is right for you right now.

Anyone can get out of control with their spending habits, bury their head in the sand, or lose focus on their priorities. Getting honest about your financial reality is the very first step toward creating the life you want.

No matter how much or how little money you have, directing it with intention is *always* a pathway to greater clarity, connection, and empowerment.

JOURNAL PROMPTS

What lifestyle level are you living at right now?

How does this feel for you here and now?

Discipline needn't feel like punishment. And an income and spending plan needn't feel harsh to be smart. The more compassionate we are with ourselves, the more sustainable our systems will be.

What comes up for you as you work through this exercise?

Give yourself the gift of curiosity, wonder, and joy as you play with your Money Map.

Paint it with everything you hold dear, and embroider it with stars. Infuse it with the rich, comforting aroma of dark chocolate. Make it your own.

By doing so, you will transform what might have been a dry, dusty budget into a pathway for greater self-awareness and connection with your values and your vision!

12

Charting Your Course through the Five Money Areas

These are five primary ways that we interact with money.

1. Earning and income

2. Spending and expenses

3. Saving

4. Debt repayment

5. Investing

It's not usually possible, or even ideal, to focus on all five areas all the time. When working through our financial strategy, or doing the emotional lifting, most people focus on just one or two of these areas while placing others on the back burner. This is fine, and absolutely normal. It's even better when we make those choices to prioritize, or back-burner, an area of our finances consciously and intentionally.

Focusing on expanding your earning potential for a specific period of time may enable you to focus on expanding your capacity to invest, or even giving back to your community.

Let's wade into the five money areas with a little more detail so that you can identify where you want to focus right now.

EARNING AND INCOME

Some people seem to have an innate gift for earning; it's always been easy for them to bring in as much money as they need, or even more than they need. Their "money work" focuses more on reining in spending or aligning their choices with their deepest values.

If you struggle with earning money, whether this means that it is challenging for you to achieve your Basic Needs, Comfortable, or Ultimate Lifestyle tier, know that you are not alone.

If earning more money is a priority for you right now, please know that it *is* possible. This work is multifaceted, so draw on your tools from Money Healing, Money Practices, and Money Maps. With compassion, determination, and patience, you can stretch your earning capacity.

JOURNAL PROMPTS

What is your money ceiling? What's the amount of money you haven't been able to break through—hourly, monthly, quarterly, or annually? Name it here, because it needs to be recognized.

Brainstorm creative options for bringing in more money. Even if the options feel totally "out there" or not possible, just let your creativity flow. *I've had clients negotiate raises, increase their rates, take on a second job, come up with new income streams as entrepreneurs, rent out their spare rooms on Airbnb, teach guitar lessons, or sell their old clothes online.*

Be gentle with yourself here. Stay open to possibilities and your dreams.

SPENDING AND EXPENSES

Bringing more consciousness to our spending and expenses doesn't have to be painfully restrictive—it can feel graceful and loving, not like some harsh, punishing "money diet."

There are so many different ways you can go about a "money cleanse," just like there are for a food cleanse. The temporary modifications you introduce here can be as structured or intuitive and rigid or lavish as you wish. What pulling back on your spending looks like will shift as you continue your journey, as time passes, as your circumstances change.

Remember, we make progress one step at a time.

JOURNAL PROMPTS

Would you consider scaling back to live within your Basic Needs tier for a set amount of time? How long? What would that look like?

Are you drawn to doing a money cleanse—tightening up your spending in a very intentional, self-loving way for a given period?

What might your "maximum lockdown mode" be? I consider this a period of time where I spend as little money as possible. Make this fun and light-hearted. How well could you live without spending much? What would this look like?

Brainstorm creative ways for reducing your spending/expenses. The possibilities are endless.

What will you do with the money you save at the end of the month?

SAVINGS

Saving is a muscle we can strengthen over time, but sometimes we need to focus on other strengths. At any given moment, it is up to each of us to determine our right relationship to savings. For some people, this means setting aside a certain percentage or dollar amount every week or once a month. Other folks love creating specific savings accounts for different types or intentions for saving, like for a vacation or a new car. I had a client who renamed her savings category *"Peace of Mind"* and noticed a swell of excitement and pride each time she saw that number grow.

JOURNAL PROMPTS

Are you in a position where you can add a new savings account or two right now?

If you could, what would you name these new savings accounts? (Cash Flow, Sweet Ride, For a Rainy Day, Cheers to the Future, See the World?)

DEBT REPAYMENT

Most financial gurus have a very strict view of debt. It often goes something like this: *"All debt is bad! You cannot be truly free and in debt."* Understandably, the people hearing this message who do have debt feel like failures. I'm here to tell you that we don't have to believe we're inadequate or less than because of debt. As with almost everything money-related, my personal experience has given me a far less rigid outlook on this debt thing.

Borrowing money can be incredibly supportive and, sometimes, utterly necessary. Just as we need to discern the right moments to take on debt in our lives, we must also distinguish the right timing for paying it back. As with savings, debt repayment can be done in a way and at a pace that aligns with our personal situation and values. Some months and years, it feels wonderful to aggressively pay down debt as quickly as possible. At other times we may need to slow down or even stop repayments to focus on other priorities.

JOURNAL PROMPTS

What Money Practices can you focus on here? This might look like tracking your debt carefully, making on-time payments to avoid late fees, watching interest rates.

What are you experiencing that needs Money Healing right now? Is it working with shame around the debt?

What have you been holding against yourself here? Are you ready to forgive yourself now? If your answer is yes, what might support you in that? If your answer is no, can you take some time to imagine what self-forgiveness might look and feel like here?

Does anything else need to be forgiven now? Is anything coming up for you that you're ready to let go of?

Can you rename your debt category(ies) something that inspires you to pay it back with enthusiasm and appreciation? For example, you might rename "student loan debt" "amazing education."

INVESTING

If you think investing is just about stocks and bonds or cold, hard cash; if you think it's something you couldn't possibly do until you have way more money; if you think you've got way more pressing priorities in life and money right now—I respectfully disagree.

We can invest in ourselves, our family, our business, our health, our education, our retirement fund, our peace of mind anywhere, anytime. Whenever we spend time, energy, or money, it's an investment. Ultimately, this final area of money mapping is all about deciding where you want to put your money, time, and energy—for now and for the future.

JOURNAL PROMPTS

Are your investments aligned with your values? Is it time to talk to your financial planner about this?

Do you need to find a new financial advisor who can help you review your portfolio so it's more aligned with socially responsible investing or social justice investing?

If you don't have traditional investment holdings, take some time to reflect on how and where you invest your time and energy.

When you consider things from this perspective, are your investments aligned with your values? What baby steps could you take to bring them into alignment?

It is a big project to look at and assess your three-tier Money Map and evaluate what lifestyle tier you're on, where you'd like to go, and how you want to dance with money. Once you've painted these broad brushstrokes on your canvas, every money decision you make is an opportunity to bring your vision to life in small and not-so-small ways.

Remember to close this exercise with a Body Check-In to ground yourself and process the work you've done here.

BODY CHECK-INS

Exercise #1: Before Money Interaction

I felt . . .

My thoughts, intuitions, realizations . . .

Exercise #2: During Money Interaction

I felt . . .

My thoughts, intuitions, realizations . . .

Exercise #3: After Money Interaction

I felt . . .

My thoughts, intuitions, realizations . . .

13

How to Make Good Money Decisions

As we learn to waltz along the new pathways of our Money Maps, making specific money decisions on a day-to-day basis can still be tricky territory. How do we know when to say yes with a flourish of fancy footwork? When do you decide to sit this one out and say nope or not now?

When you have a process and a set of questions to support you in making solid money decisions, you can feel clear and empowered with each one you make. We won't always get it right or even close sometimes—never mind perfect. Please remember that we are all here to learn, grow, adjust, and fine-tune all the time. The work is ongoing as our journey unfolds.

I remember when I first started coming up with questions to ask myself while browsing the local thrift store, shopping online, heading into Target, or standing in the middle of a car dealership. Having a set of questions to ask was so helpful to my decision-making process. They truly make all the difference. I don't feel like I'm making decisions in the dark, guessing through it, or relying only on my emotions.

I'm human—sometimes I forget to go through the questions in the moment. When that happens, I cut myself some slack and make a point of reviewing my purchases afterward. As I've integrated this practice, I have found that combining Body Checks-Ins with a great set of questions has significantly impacted how I make money decisions.

I have a little ritual now: I do a Body Check-In before, during, and after my money interaction. I ask my questions during the purchase moment, and afterward, I review how it went, what I learned, and what I could do differently the next time I find myself in a similar situation.

I want to share one of my favorite, simple frameworks with you, one that I use all the time when making small, medium, and large spending decisions. Let's build a set of questions that you can use when faced with a money decision, no matter the size.

There is no single "right" way to make a money decision; we must all create our own criteria, reflecting and honoring what matters most to us at each point in our lives. I'm excited to share this simple tool to support you as you grow along your money journey.

Use the space provided to write down the questions *you* want to reflect on whenever you need to make a money decision—whether at the grocery store or considering a much larger, and maybe more exciting, purchase.

SMALL MONEY DECISIONS

Here we reflect on what you would consider to be minor purchases—perhaps picking up a few items at Target or perusing the clothes at your favorite thrift store.

Before
Do a Body Check-In and then consider:

Am I hungry, angry, lonely, or tired? (You can think of this as HALT for short. The HALT acronym comes out of recovery programs, but adding this awareness can help all of us make better decisions.)

Check-In: How am I feeling? How might I take care of myself before making this smaller money choice?

During
What questions do you want to have in mind while you're shopping or considering your smaller purchases?

Why do I want this?

Do I need it?

How often will I actually use it?

Am I going to enjoy it by the time I get home?

What emotion am I hoping this purchase will create for me?

Am I trying to impress someone?

Am I trying to care for someone or myself with this purchase?

How does this purchase align with my short- and long-term goals?

Use the space below to brainstorm your questions:

After

Now take a few moments to gauge how you're feeling about the purchase you've made. This is an exercise in growing your self-awareness and bringing that gentle attention to your relationship with money. Come back to your questions and follow up with yourself. Was this a good money decision?

Again, you'll want to craft your own questions, but here are a few to start:

How do I feel in my body?

Do I feel energized or drained by this interaction?

What emotions are coming up for me now?

How will I know if I've made a good money decision?

What would I do differently next time?

Use the space below to write down your experience post-purchase.

Revisit down the Road

Am I getting value from this purchase?

Am I enjoying it?

When I reflect on this purchase, how do I feel in my body?

MEDIUM MONEY DECISIONS

Here we create space to consciously examine midsize money decisions. Consider expenditures such as buying a car, computer, furniture, new appliances, or planning a big trip.

Before
Do a Body Check-In and then consider:

Am I hungry, angry, lonely, or tired? (You can think of this as HALT for short. The HALT acronym comes out of recovery programs, but adding this awareness can help all of us make better decisions.)

Check-In: How am I feeling? How might I take care of myself before making this medium-size money choice? What tools or resources would make me feel better supported in making this decision?

During
Why do I want this?

Do I need it?

What value do I anticipate getting out of this purchase?

What emotion am I hoping this purchase will create for me?

Am I trying to impress someone?

Am I trying to care for someone or myself with this purchase?

Is this purchase aligned with my values and the things that truly matter to me?

How does this purchase align with my short- and long-term goals?

How does this fit in with my yearly cash flow? With my two-year plan?

Use the space below to brainstorm your questions:

After

Now take a few moments to gauge how you're feeling about the purchase.

Again, you'll want to craft your own questions, but here are a few to start:

How do I feel in my body?

Do I feel energized or drained by this interaction?

What emotions are coming up for me now?

Use the space below to write down your experience immediately or soon after purchase.

Revisit down the Road

What benefit or value am I getting from this purchase?

What emotions are coming up for me around this now?

When I reflect on this choice, how do I feel in my body?

LARGE MONEY DECISIONS

Here we are examining large money decisions. These choices are significant in our lives and our finances. Here we are thinking along the lines of buying a house or planning a wedding.

While there are many other large money decisions we make throughout our lives, choices like starting a business, taking a sabbatical, or deciding when to retire require more long-term planning and the personalized support of a financial planner or coach—or both! This is a gentle reminder that we all need to seek guidance and support in these big-picture money decisions—and that asking for help is both brave and empowering.

In the meantime, the questions below will help guide you as you encounter large money decisions in your day-to-day life, bringing more authenticity and intimacy to your relationship with money.

Before

Do a Body Check-In and then consider:

Am I hungry, angry, lonely, or tired? (You can think of this as HALT for short. The HALT acronym comes out of recovery programs, but adding this awareness can help all of us make better decisions.)

Use the space below to check in with yourself. How am I feeling? How might I take care of myself before making this money choice? What tools or resources would make me feel better prepared and supported in this decision?

During

Would I call this purchase a need, a want, or a desire?

What value do I expect from this decision?

Is this purchase accessible for me right now? Do I have the cash flow for this?

Does this purchase support me in my short- and long-term goals?

At this point, will this stretch me in an unsustainable way?

How does this fit in with my cash flow and life plan in the next two years?

Does this purchase contribute to my dream or detract from it? Or is it neutral?

In this particular moment of my life, which lifestyle tier does this purchase fall under? Is it Basic Needs, Comfortable, or Ultimate?

Does this particular purchase align with my values and what truly matters to me?

The After-Purchase Review

Take a few moments to gauge how you're feeling about your purchase.

Again, you'll want to craft your own questions, but here are a few to start:

How do I feel in my body?

Do I feel energized or drained by this money interaction?

What emotions are coming up for me now?

Use the space below to write down your experience post-purchase.

You can always refer back to these questions, revising them over time as needed. Anytime you feel a big money decision coming up for you, keep these questions in mind. Give yourself space and time to revisit and explore your answers to ground yourself and the choices you make along your money journey.

14

Handling Money Curveballs

There are ebbs and flows in life and money.

What do you do when you hit a wall when it comes to money?

What do you do when you're not just stuck—you're up-to-your-elbows-in-molasses *stuck*? You keep asking the same questions, and you're getting nowhere, only more confused. And that creative positivity you're known for? Must be on vacation.

You are not broken or beyond redemption. It happens to all of us. This is what it feels like to be in the middle of a "money curveball."

It could be that you just found out you're being audited by the IRS. Or you haven't gotten a raise in a few years, and you're feeling it. Maybe you're going through a big cash flow dip as an entrepreneur. Perhaps you're trying to decide if you should sell your home to downsize your expenses. It could be that you have a big dream trip that you don't have the funding for—yet. Or a global pandemic has you living in lockdown, your options are limited, and you find yourself struggling emotionally and financially.

The bad news? This can be uncomfortable and overwhelming.

The good news? There really are ways to work through it and come out the other side at least a smidgen more financially enlightened!

Now, I know we all hope that one day we will be done with this money thing. We'll get it all figured out and live happily ever after with all that money stuff blissfully resolved. But, really, our relationship with money is ongoing. This journey is lifelong.

There will always be money curveballs, just like there are curveballs in life.

What happens when we find ourselves in the middle of a money riddle? A lot of us freak out. In an instant, we are ready to fight, take flight, or freeze.

The good news? There are tools to help you work through your money curveballs when they strike.

Facing a big money challenge head-on and with an open heart can increase one's courage in so many areas of life.

We *can* find new solutions, new possibilities, and new ways to work around money, even when we are stressed and the pressure feels incredibly high.

In my own life, I certainly have my stuck moments, crying moments, and moments when I just can't find the key to unlock a money riddle . . . until, suddenly, I do.

When the answer comes, it's magic—I'm incredibly grateful that I have finally broken through and found a remedy. Like the framework I sought in the woods, walking, praying, and bargaining with the sky so many years ago, suddenly, I'm able to see a whole new way to do something that solves my money riddle.

Hard work, intention, perseverance, some prayer, and a little magic set the money curveball right. It reminds me of a great quote usually attributed to Albert Einstein: "*Insanity is doing the same thing over and over again and expecting different results.*"

Our money journey calls us to keep sitting with our money riddles until we solve them and find a new pathway to embark upon our next adventure.

WAYS TO WORK WITH A MONEY CURVEBALL

We all deal with money challenges in life. Believe it or not, everyone encounters those big money curveballs that, at first glance, we don't know how to manage. Here is a simple but effective framework to help you move through these trials when they come your way.

JOURNAL PROMPTS FOR MONEY CURVEBALLS

Take a deep breath and get comfy in your space. Do a Body Check-In before you get started with the following prompts.

Allow yourself to think back over your life until a particular money curveball comes to mind. Describe the situation in detail here:

What emotions are coming up for you as you write about this situation? Explore those and let everything out here.

What's happening in your body? What sensations do you notice? Are you feeling fight, flight, or freeze?

Take a deep breath. How can you reach out for support?

Begin to brainstorm new questions to ask yourself surrounding this money curveball.

Start by filling in these sentences as fast as you can, as many times as you can:

"I wonder if . . ."

"I wonder if I could . . ."

"I wonder if they could . . ."

"I wonder if we could . . ."

Give yourself space to wonder freely/brainstorm below:

Looking at what you wrote, what is the *very next* baby step you could take to move forward? It could be sharing your situation with a trusted person or taking a walk in nature to think.

Below, write one to three baby steps you could possibly take after that:

If you are feeling some resistance, use this space to explore why and how you might move through it:

Once you've taken a baby step, or three, report back here. How did it go? Did any of your next steps become clear as a result? How do you feel?

With patience, gentleness, and abundant self-love, we make our way—one tiny baby step at a time.

Experiment with this framework. See if it helps you move through—and resolve—your next big money challenge with greater ease.

- What money riddle are you facing right now? (Acknowledging, naming, and admitting that you're dealing with a curveball are *huge*.)

- Share all your money feelings that are coming up during this challenge—describe them in detail. What do they bring up for you? Are there past triggers here?

- What new questions can you start to ask yourself? Brainstorm new ways of looking at your curveballs just like I did above!

- What type of additional support do you need right now to move through this riddle?

- What friends or trusted people can you talk to as you work through this money conundrum?

We rarely welcome money curveballs, but they are always an opportunity for growth—if we seize them. If you're grappling with a major money riddle right now? Keep going. Keep sitting with it. Find the grit deep down inside of you to stick with it, no matter what. The answer will come to you, whether it takes days, weeks, months, or years. No matter how stuck you feel, you will eventually find a solution if you sit with it long enough.

Know that. Trust it. You'll eventually see that your curveball is a door and you can unlock it. You *will step* through that doorway into a space of intuitive, financial enlightenment. And who knows what you might discover or inspire along the way? I've seen it happen time and again in my own life and over and over in my thousands-strong Art of Money community.

I know you've got this. Keep going.

15

Your Money Legacy

A Money Legacy is everything you pass on that is related to money, including how you lived your life. It's the wealth you accumulate, your attitudes about money, and everything that money meant to you.

If it helps, consider these questions through the lens of the practical, emotional-psychological, and spiritual perspectives.

LOOKING AHEAD JOURNAL PROMPTS

What is an important nugget of money wisdom you'd like to pass on to your own children—or the next generation?

What financial practices, insights, and attitudes have genuinely worked for you? What would you love to leave behind?

Is there any money shame that you need to heal to make sure you don't pass it on? *Honestly, I believe we all have these!* Are there any money messes or loose ends you want to tie up?

What have you learned about earning, spending, saving, giving, and receiving that you think could benefit others to know?

When it comes to money, what do you want to be remembered for?

What attitudes toward money would you want to pass on or model for future generations?

Finally, take action.

Is there anything you feel called to do to help bring your Money Legacy to life in a tangible way? Do you want to hire an estate planner and set up a will or trust? Do you want to have a conversation with your children, partner, or friends about money?

What tiny day-to-day things can you do to breathe life into your Money Legacy right now? For example, if generosity is a part of the Money Legacy you'd like to leave, be on the lookout for ways to show it.

> As you look forward to the legacy you'd like to leave, remember to bring generous doses of gentleness, curiosity, compassion, and self-love to the process.

Like everything around money, these questions touch upon so many aspects of you. Here we integrate your health and body, emotions, beliefs, relationships, gender dynamics, nuts and bolts practices, big visioning, deep soul diving, and so much more.

Personally, one of my biggest money riddles has been learning to think of the future. Until my early thirties, I couldn't even conceive of my finances more than a few weeks ahead. Like so many Americans, I was living paycheck to paycheck, and even imagining life down the road felt like a luxury I couldn't afford.

The way someone thinks about their financial future reveals a lot about their personality, too. You may be a dreamer with rose-colored glasses or a gloom-and-doom type, or you might experience the future as I once did—as an unfathomable blank canvas beyond your imagination.

My challenge is to stretch into my ability to think about the future so I can prioritize and plan for it and start taking action steps now to provide for it. Future planning brings us face-to-face with our relationship to trust, optimism, and darkness. It also reveals the tricky balance between present-moment well-being and the contingencies we may not think to expect for later.

> One of our life lessons is to learn how to appreciate the now while also working toward future goals.

We all need to find our own solutions for the now vs. future equation, but openly asking the questions is, in my mind, a major victory—and one worth celebrating!

The question of Money Legacy brings us directly to the future's doorstep. You might choose to sock money away in stocks and investments for your retirement or your children's future goals and dreams. You may focus on philanthropy as the gift you'll pass down to the next generation. The attitudes and choices you embody during your life will create your Money Legacy.

My hope is that my legacy strikes a balance between honoring the past, present-moment self-care, and lovingly caretaking for the future. I haven't found that delicate balance yet, so I keep bringing my questions to my heart and my bookkeeping.

We all have growing edges as we travel along our money journey. Thankfully, the more we explore our money relationship, the deeper our reserves of self-trust become.

REVIEW AND REFLECT

Reflection on a journey begun:

How would you describe your current relationship with money? Reflect on where you've been and where you are—what has changed since you've started bringing more attention to your relationship with money?

What areas of your money relationship need some TLC? What are your growing edges or stuck places? Name them here.

Do you have a weekly Money Practice now? What does this look like for you? What thoughts come up for you around this? Are you loving it or resisting it? How does it feel?

What's the next level for you—emotionally, practically, or spiritually—with money? For example: Are you adding new financial support people to your team? Are you learning QuickBooks for the first time? Are you beginning to track your spending and income with a bookkeeping system? Are you working on receiving in a new way?

What are your goals right now for the next six months to a year when it comes to money? Where do you want to be in six months? What do you want to accomplish or get done? Heal or shift? Where do you want to dive deeper?

What boundaries do you want to put into place as you move forward?

What are you grateful for? How will you celebrate the things that bring you gratitude in your everyday life?

Remember, this journey is yours to enjoy.
It isn't a sprint, and the finish line isn't as important
as the experience. You can take the whole process
as luxuriously slow or lighthearted as you like.

A Letter in Closing

I am honored to meet you here, dear Money Adventurer.

Wherever you stand in your money journey at this very moment, however your path is unfolding, it is a privilege to share this work with you.

And let me be clear—this is not the end.

Your personal Money Story continues as you do, baby step by brave leap. Sometimes we find ourselves stumbling in the shadows. If you're struggling to find your stride, please trust me when I say that it will come. I find myself there too, sometimes, even after all these years.

The pursuit of authenticity and genuine connection can get uncomfortable. Growth, forgiveness, letting go—these waters run deep. We may find ourselves spending more time in a shadowy valley than we hoped or expected. You are worth the heavy lifting. Your heart deserves the excavation. You can write a new chapter, and you will. You've already begun.

Take a deep breath. Do a Body Check-In.

Now, cut yourself some slack and allow yourself to rest in grace. Curl up with a cozy cuppa and some tantalizing dark chocolate—or whatever it is that makes you feel uplifted and loved.

I invite you to revisit your journaling and the work you've done here when you need guidance, when you want to celebrate, as you choose to rest and reflect along the way. Or check in when that still, small voice calls you to gratitude as you swim through new depths of intimacy and self-knowing or when you're confronted with difficult emotions as you navigate a significant money decision. Allow this workbook to serve as a trail marker, a safe space to return to when you need to collect your bearings, a grounding point as you shift patterns and move mountains.

Thank you for allowing me to be part of your journey.

Resources to Support You Further

I sincerely hope this workbook has helped you explore one of the most important relationships of your life. Remember, your relationship with money truly needs consistent care and nourishment. A healthy, peaceful, empowered financial life is made up of *sooooo* many teeny, tiny baby steps.

In this workbook, I've introduced you to some of the most important Money Practices in my financial tool kit. From Body Check-Ins to your Money Story, Money Dates, and your three-tier Money Map—each of these is a powerful vehicle for growth and healing. Any one of these, all alone, can transform your money relationship right here and now, if you let it.

However, what you've experienced here is just a small sample of a huge body of work. This workbook is the tip of the Art of Money iceberg. There are many topics and tools not covered here, such as:

- Going deeper with the somatic tools

- Choosing which bookkeeping system to use (Mint, YNAB, Quicken, MoneyGrit, QuickBooks)

- Learning how to use your bookkeeping system (DIY or with a bookkeeping trainer)

- Creating your "un-scary" chart of accounts

- Learning how to have monthly, quarterly, and annual Money Dates

- Clarifying the different players on a financial support team (bookkeepers, accountants, financial therapists, financial coaches, financial planners, etc.)

- How to choose and hire *your* financial support team

- Understanding couples' money dynamics

- Learning a framework for Couples' Money Dates

- Understanding your money dynamics with your parents and your kids

- Understanding how to have healthier money conversations with your spouse, parents, children, and friends

- Setting your rates, learning the best business model, and managing your money as a creative entrepreneur

- How to make a good money decision—on your own and as a couple

- Learning the language of investments

- Learning how to invest your money with SRI's—Socially Responsible Investments

- Learning how to budget and understand your cash flow

- Deeper personal finance, couples finance, and creative entrepreneur money teachings

- How to make big money decisions like taking a sabbatical, starting a business, or planning for retirement—a big process that involves weaving together your numbers, resources, visioning, goals, plans, and phase of life with deep consideration and support

- Understanding the macro side of money and the grand, sweeping systems that frame our lives, like the influence and impositions of global economics and world history—from the wealth gap and socioeconomic structures that marginalize communities to social justice and the redistribution of resources

If this list seems like a lot, that's because it is! As you live your life, you'll continue to deepen your knowledge and understanding of money, and I invite you to continue to explore that relationship with me in the Art of Money program or book.

In gratitude,

About the Author

Bari Tessler, MA, is a financial therapist and founder of the Art of Money, a yearlong money school. Before creating her own Financial Therapy methodology in 2001, she started her career as a somatic therapist. Her first book, *The Art of Money: A Life-Changing Guide to Financial Happiness*, was published in 2016. Bari lives with her husband, son, and many cats in Boulder, Colorado.